15

a perfect fit

a perfect fit

Create personalised patterns for a limitless wardrobe

Lynne Garner

David and Charles

www.mycraftivity.com

To Mrs Tingle and Mrs H (Joan), whose teaching skills and patience created a lifelong love of all things sewing. Thank you.

David & Charles books are available from all good bookshops; alternatively you can contact our Orderline on 0870 9908222 or write to us at: FREEPOST EX2 110, D&C Direct, Newton Abbot, TQ12 4ZZ (no stamp required UK only); US customers call 800-289-0963 and Canadian customers call 800-840-5220.

A DAVID & CHARLES BOOK

David & Charles is an F+W Media Inc. company
4700 East Galbraith Road, Cincinnati, OH 45236

First published in the UK in 2009
Copyright © 2009 Breslich & Foss Ltd

Photography: Dominic Harris
Jacket and page 4 photography: Ruth Jenkinson
Design: Louise Leffler   Design concept: Bookworx
Illustrations: Stephen Dew

Conceived and produced by Breslich & Foss Ltd
Unit 2A Union Court, 20–22 Union Road, London SW4 6JP

A catalogue record for this book is available from the British Library

ISBN-13: 978-0-7153-3517-8
ISBN-10: 0-7153-3517-0

Printed in China for David & Charles
Brunel House   Newton Abbot   Devon
Visit our website at www.davidandcharles.co.uk

10 9 8 7 6 5 4 3 2 1

Contents

introduction

I have taught patterncutting, dressmaking and sewing in colleges for more years than I would like to admit, and during that time I have found that most, if not all, of my students have had to adapt shop-bought garment patterns in order to make them fit properly.

Commercial patterns are cut to 'standard' sizes and they just don't allow for us being slightly bigger around the bust, or smaller on the hips, or slightly longer in the arms, or having a longer back length (which is my main problem), than is considered 'standard'. They also do not allow for 'figure faults' – which is actually a term I really don't like. These are not 'faults' but differences we should be proud of. What a boring world this would be if we were all 'standard'.

As a result of these discrepancies between patterns and people, I found myself teaching pattern adaption more and more often. I also discovered that my students (like me) really didn't like the process of drafting (drawing) a flat block using measurements and maths. However, they really enjoyed the hands-on process of draping, a process I was taught as a student and just loved.

So it seemed a natural progression for me to teach my students how to drape, then how to turn this calico block into a paper block. This block could then be used to create personalised patterns that fitted perfectly and allowed for those little differences that make all our figures individual.

Draping a basic block with calico also had the benefit of no longer having to deal with the horrendous sums you have to do to create a paper block using the mathematical method. Even armed with a pocket calculator I used to have to take a deep breath before tackling a basic bodice block. If you've ever drafted a block straight onto paper using body measurements and maths, you'll know what I mean.

Traditionally, draping is the method used by couturiers to create the fabulous *haute couture* clothes that you see in the catwalk shows of all the major fashion houses. Fitting models would be used to drape the catwalk garment on, then a pattern would be made and every woman who ordered the garment would have it personally fitted on her. This goes some way to explaining why couture clothes are so expensive, and why they look so amazing.

It is a simplified version of this traditional draping method that I taught my students, a method that was easy to master and allowed for all the different figures types. This enabled students to create a block that was 'theirs', and which took into consideration each little bump those unlucky 'standard' people don't have. Armed with these basic blocks my students were able to create patterns and sew clothes that really did fit.

In this book you will find all my years of teaching experience illustrated in step-by-step guides that show you exactly how you, too, can drape calico to make your own blocks. I then take you through the stages of creating paper blocks and adapting these into patterns from which you can make stylish garments.

I have designed a selection of tops, sleeves, skirts, trousers and dresses with instructions and pattern diagrams that show you how to adjust your blocks to make them. Once you have made a few of these I'm sure you'll want to design your own garments and sew those. So find a friend, get pinning and start to create garments that are a perfect fit.

LYNNE GARNER

'Create personalised patterns that fit perfectly and allow for those little differences that make all our figures individual to us.'

getting Started

To help you create your own mix-and-match wardrobe, this chapter includes some basic information that will help you create wearable, professional-looking garments time and time again.

Measuring your body
How to take the necessary measurements accurately.

Tools and equipment
A list of the basic equipment you will need.

Working with fabrics
An introduction to fabric types available to the home sewer, their qualities and tips for sewing them, plus a guide to working out quantities required for patterns.

Basic sewing techniques
The basic techniques you need to master in order to sew garments that you'll want to wear.

measuring your body

You need to measure your body to prepare calico for draping your personalised fabric blocks (see pages 30–49). Once you have your blocks you will want to adapt them to make the patterns on pages 64–113. Then, once you have grown in confidence, you will want to make garments to your own designs. Here are the basic measurements needed for everything you may make and how to take them.

1 Bust
This measurement is taken around the fullest part of the bust.

2 Waist
This is taken around the natural waistline. To find the natural waistline, tie a ribbon around the waist and roll the body from side to side, the ribbon will settle on the natural waistline.

3 Back width
Measure down 10cm (4 in) from the prominent bone at the base of the neck. From this measured point, measure across the back from arm to arm, where the shoulder seams of a garment would be.

4 Front width
At the same height as for Back Width (see 3), measure from arm to arm across the chest.

5 Back length to waist
Measure from the prominent bone at the base of the neck to the natural waistline (see 2).

6 Shoulder length
Measure from the base of the neck, at the side, to the shoulder point – where a shoulder seam would be.

7 Hips
Measure around the widest part of the hips, which on most figure types is around 22.75cm (9 in) below the natural waistline (see 2).

8 Skirt length
Measure from the natural waistline (see 2) to the desired skirt length.

9 Trouser length
Taken from the waistline (see 2) to the required length of the trousers. Usually this is on the prominent bone of the ankle, but length can be adjusted to suit fashion and taste.

10 Armhole measurement
This is the only measurement taken directly from your bodice block. Run the tape measure around the front and back armholes on your bodice block (without any seam allowances) and add these figures together.

11 Sleeve length
Hold the arm slightly out from your side and bend it, then run the tape measure along the outside edge from where the shoulder seam of a garment would be down to the wrist. Usually the bone on the wrist is used as a landmark, but if you prefer a slightly longer sleeve, then add the extra length required now.

12 Upper arm width
Bend the arm and measure around the broadest part of the upper arm: place a finger under the tape measure to ensure that the finished sleeve is not too tight.

13 Wrist
Measure around the wrist, placing a finger under the tape measure to ensure that the finished sleeve is not too tight.

14 Body rise
Sit down on a hard surface and measure from the natural waistline (see 2) to the surface.

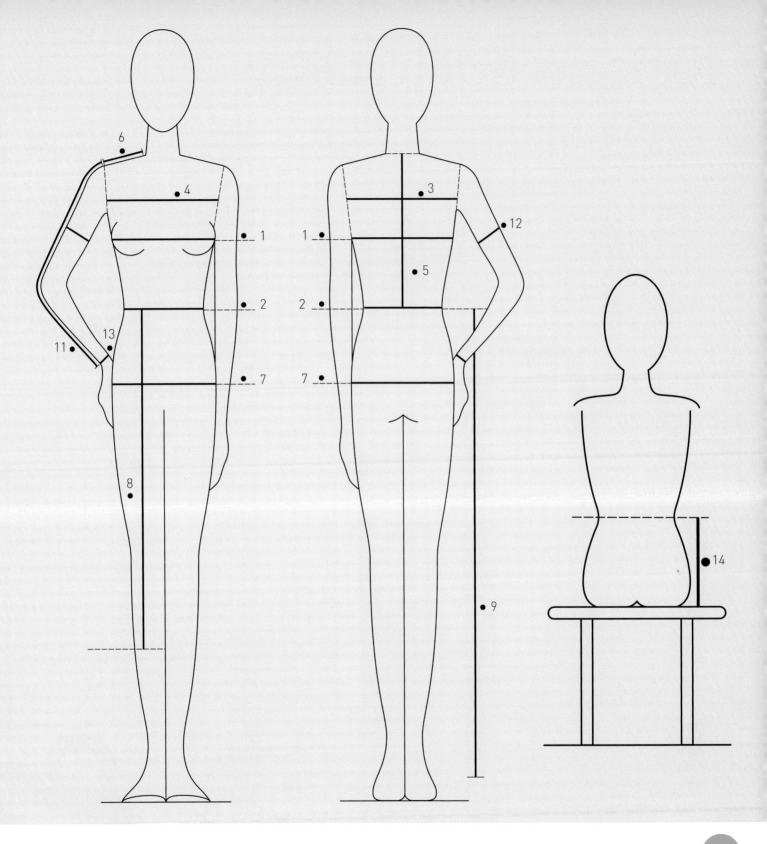

tools and equipment

You only need a limited amount of inexpensive equipment for draping calico to make blocks and then turning these fabric blocks into paper patterns.

Draping equipment

Tightly fitting top and trousers
The person being draped upon will need to wear a tightly fitting top and trousers that can be pinned onto.

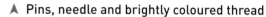

▲ Tape measure
A good-quality, plastic-coated tape measure will be needed to take the body measurements and to transfer these measurements onto the calico before you start the draping process.

▲ Pins, needle and brightly coloured thread
To prepare the calico for the draping process, you will need to tack some design lines and these are best done using brightly coloured thread. If you are draping the bodice, skirt and sleeve in one session (as we have in this book), you will need a large number of good-quality, fine pins.

◀ Fabric marker or pencil
Once the draping process is complete, but before you remove the calico from the body, you will need to draw in all the seams and darts. If you do not have a fabric marker, then an ordinary drawing pencil can be used.

▼ Scissors
You will need large scissors for cutting both paper and fabric and small fabric scissors. Don't ruin your fabric scissors by cutting paper with them: tie a strip of fabric to the handle so that the rest of the family don't use them for their papercrafts.

▼ Calico
Use light- to mediumweight calico with a tight weave for draping your blocks. This is both forgiving and will not stretch too much during the draping process.

Paper pattern-making equipment

◄ **Drafting paper or dot-and-cross paper**
Drafting paper is a large sheet of paper that is very similar to tracing paper, or paper that has dots and crosses printed on it at 2.5cm (1 in) intervals. Both are available on the roll (which is very economical if you intend creating all your own patterns), or in packs, often of three or five folded sheets.

◄ **Ruler**
A plastic or metal ruler for drawing straight lines for darts and other elements. A long thin metre (yard) rule, available in many sewing or office supply shops, is useful for drawing longer lines for skirts and trousers.

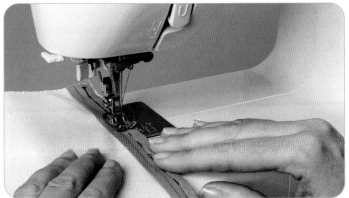

Optional equipment

If you are not very confident when it comes to drawing out your paper patterns, then you may find these two bits of equipment useful.

Set square
Available from most good office supply or art shops, this helps you to draw neat and accurate patterns with angles of 90 degrees where needed.

Flexible curve rule
This item is often used by crafters from knitters to wood workers. It has a vinyl outer skin with a lead core that can be bent into any shape you wish. It allows you to create curves with ease and comes in a variety of different lengths.

▲ **Sewing machine**
A new sewing machine can be an expensive purchase, but you don't need many of the features more costly machines have. The features you do need are:
● Straight stitch that can be altered in length
● Zigzag stitch that can be altered in width
● A buttonhole-making facility – my preferred option is a one-step buttonhole
● Ability to drop the feed dog (the teeth below the foot)
● A free-arm function, this makes sewing items such as cuffs and sleeves much easier
● A cover to keep machine clean while it is not in use
● A selection of feet – zigzag, straight stitch, buttonhole (if there is a one-step function) and zip feet

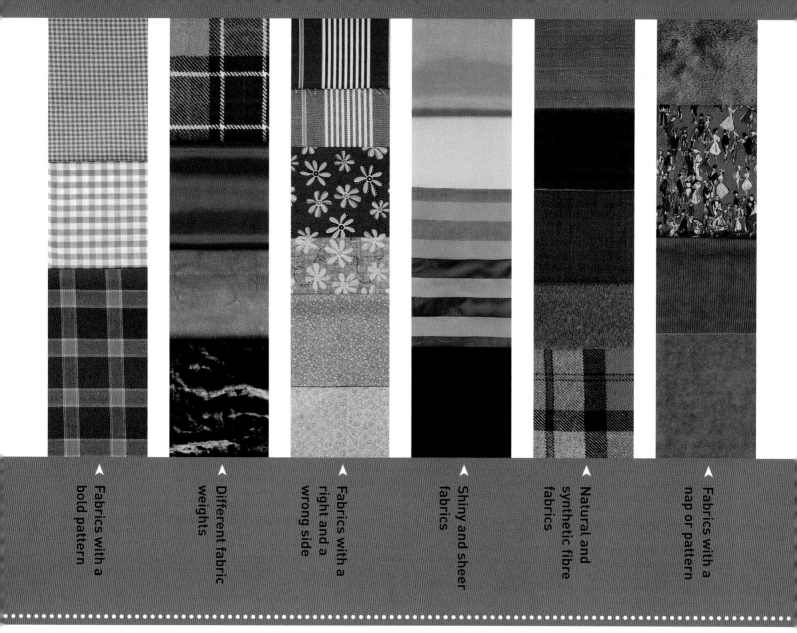

Fabrics with a bold pattern

Different fabric weights

Fabrics with a right and a wrong side

Shiny and sheer fabrics

Natural and synthetic fibre fabrics

Fabrics with a nap or pattern

Working with fabrics

There is a huge variety of different fabrics available to the dressmaker and each one has its own uses and properties. Here is an overview of the most common types and a few hints and tips that will make it easier to choose the right fabric for your project.

Fabrics with a bold pattern

With fabrics such as checks, ensure that the design runs around the whole body for a more professional finish.

Lay one piece of the pattern – for example, the front bodice – on the fabric and trace a few of the check lines onto the pattern piece. Remove the pattern piece and line it up against the back bodice pattern piece. Extend the traced design lines onto the back bodice. When laying out the pattern pieces, simply match up the traced lines on the patterns with the checks.

Alternatively, pick a dominant line in the pattern and line this up with, for example, the waistline on all the relevant pattern pieces.

Different fabric weights

Fabric comes in a wide range of weights from the lightest tulle to heavyweight denim and you do need to consider this when sewing. Change the sewing machine needle to suit the weight of the fabric you are sewing: for example, for lighter weight fabrics use a needle size 11–14 (80–90) and for heavier weight fabrics use a needle size 14–18 (90–110).

Also, you may well find that you need to adjust the tension on your sewing machine. It is always a good idea to sew a small test seam on two scraps of fabric to check the stitch tension and then adjust it as needed before starting the project.

Fabrics with a right and a wrong side

Fabrics such as printed cotton, cord, velvet, or a woven fabric with an integral design, will have a right and a wrong side: this is often referred to in patterns as the RS (right side) and WS (wrong side).

With these fabrics it is very important to ensure that you cut out a left-hand and a right-hand pattern piece. If you fold the fabric in half with the right sides together, you are sure to cut a left-hand and a right-hand piece out at the same time.

However, if you cut just one layer of fabric at a time, remember to flip the pattern piece over before cutting out the second fabric piece.

Shiny and sheer fabrics

Many shiny fabrics pin-hole easily, so invest in fine pins and always pin within the seam allowance – any holes will then be lost inside the seam.

For fabrics that water-mark, never use a damp cloth or spray on water directly while pressing. Test a scrap of fabric before pressing the garment.

If shiny fabric moves around when you are cutting pieces out, then cut all the pieces from a single layer.

If the fabric does not feed smoothly through your sewing machine, then place a sheet of tissue paper beneath it. This can be gently pulled away from the stitches when the seam is finished. Some fabrics will snag when sewing, so use a ball point needle in your machine instead of a standard sewing needle.

Natural and synthetic fibre fabrics

Fabrics are made from a range of both natural fibres (including wool, silk, linen and cotton) and man-made fibres (including rayon, polyester, terylene and lycra).

Wool has a tendency to shrink so always pre-shrink the fabric by steaming it on a smooth surface before you cut out the pieces. However, wool becomes soft when warm, so allow it to cool before you move it.

Some cotton fabrics fray badly, so finish the seams using an overlocker or zigzag stitch. On a lightweight fabric you can use bias binding (see page 28) to create a very neat finish.

Because synthetic fabrics do not breathe, try to avoid them if you are making a garment for summer wear.

Fabrics with a nap or pattern

Fabrics that have a nap (also called 'pile') include fur, cord and velvet. Stroke the fabric to feel which is the 'up' and which is the 'down' of the nap.

Always have the nap running down the body on all pattern pieces. This means that you can't lay the pattern pieces in different directions on the fabric as the 'down' nap may be shinier than the 'up' nap resulting in the garment looking as though it was in two shades of the colour. Also, the pile running up the body tends to make the wearer look larger.

Fabrics with an all-over print must be laid out with the design the right way up on each piece. If your fabric has a nap or pattern, then allow extra (see Calculating Fabric Quantities, page 17).

Choosing interfacing

Most garments will need interfacing somewhere; to give a neat and professional finish to collars and cuffs, or to add body to a jacket. Choosing the correct interfacing can make or break the finish of your garment, so here are some helpful tips.

For sheer ease and speed, iron-on interfacing beats sew-in interfacing hands down. However, there are some fabrics, such as silk, where it is better to use the sew-in type because the iron-on interfacing can affect the look of the fabric.

Do test iron-on interfacing on a scrap piece of the fabric first. This allows you to work out what setting you need to have the iron at and the optimum amount of time needed to press the interfacing in place. Also, do check the manufacturer's instructions as brands do vary a little.

When fusing the interfacing to the fabric, press it on in small sections (lifting and replacing the iron), rather than ironing it in place (moving the iron backwards and forwards on the fabric), as this can move the interfacing.

Iron-on interfacing can be very messy if you accidentally iron the wrong side. Always check that the glue side is facing the fabric: often holding it under an angled light will allow you to see the small glue dots clearly. Get it the wrong way up and you'll have to spend the next hour cleaning your iron.

Also, cover the surface of your ironing board so that if the interfacing does go over the edge of your fabric, it will not ruin the surface of your board.

Once you have interfaced the pattern piece, roll it and then pull on the fabric slightly. If the interfacing lifts then it has not stuck properly and you will have to iron it again.

Choose interfacing to suit the section of garment you are working on. You do not have to use the same weight or type of interfacing throughout the entire garment, so mix and match as appropriate. For example, you may choose a heavier weight interfacing for a mandarin collar on a shirt than you do for the cuffs.

Generally you should use an interfacing that is slightly lighter in weight than the fabric. If you find it is too light then you can always attach a second layer for a little more stiffness.

Pick an interfacing that acts in the same way as the fabric you are working on: if you need to interface a knitted fabric, then pick knitted fusible interfacing that stretches. There are two types of this, one that stretches

from selvage to selvage and another that stretches in both directions.

When cutting out pieces of woven interfacing, ensure that the direction of the weave is running in the same direction as the weave on the fabric pattern piece.

When working with heavyweight interfacings, cut them without the seam allowances to reduce any bulk on the seams.

Not all interfacing is white, so if you are working on a dark fabric then try to source a black interfacing. If you are working on a light-coloured fabric, then use white interfacing.

Calculating fabric quantities

When you buy a pattern you will be provided with all the relevant information, including how much fabric will be required. However, when you are creating your own designs you have to work out this information for yourself.

In order to calculate how much fabric you need, you will need to know the width of the fabric you are going to use. Fabrics come in standard widths (always approximate) of 90cm (36 in), 114cm (45 in), 138cm (54 in) and 150cm (60 in).

If you have not chosen a fabric, then you need to work out the amount needed for each of the widths listed. This may seem time-consuming, but it's quicker (and cheaper) than going to the fabric shop, guessing the quantity, getting home, realising it's wrong and going back to the shop.

Never use the fabric selvage as part of your garment. It does not act in the same way as the main body of the fabric and may warp, shrink or pucker once it has been washed. So, when laying out your pattern pieces allow 2.5cm (1 in) along the selvage edge.

When working with a fabric that has a nap or a repeat pattern (see page 15), you will have to allow extra fabric so that you can match the pattern. It is advisable to allow at least two extra pattern repeats to do this.

1 Designate an edge of a large table as the fold of the fabric and place a metre (yard) rule across the table at right angles to this edge.

2 Using pieces of masking tape, mark off half the width of your fabric; for example, 75cm (30 in) if you are going to use 150-cm (60-in) wide fabric.

3 Lay the pattern pieces out following the markings. So, place the centre front section along the 'fold' edge of the table. Start with the larger pieces of the garment and position them to best advantage. Then place the smaller pattern pieces – such as pockets and collars – between them.

(see page 15)

picking the right fabric

When making your own garments it is sometimes difficult to decide which fabric would be suitable. To help you make the correct choice you can:

- Look at the back of a shop-bought pattern envelope for a similar pattern, because they often give a list of suitable fabrics.

- Look in clothes shops to see if there is a similar garment to the one you wish to make and read the label to find out what fabric has been used.

- Ask yourself what use is the garment going to be put to? If it is for the office, then go for something a little heavier, but the same dress made in a shiny silk fabric is ideal as a little party dress.

- Ask yourself what time of year you are making the garment for? Light cottons are great for the warmer months while woollen fabrics are best for the winter.

4 Once all the pattern pieces are in position, measure how much of the table length you have used. This will give you the amount of fabric you will need.

basic sewing techniques

There are some basic sewing techniques required to complete the range of garments in this book. We have chosen the simplest, and usually the speediest, methods that will give a good result. If you are a dressmaking novice, then just take your time and practise on scrap fabric first.

Cutting out fabric pieces

Open seam

Stay stitching

Tailor's tacks

Sewing darts

Setting in a fitted sleeve

Setting in a gathered sleeve

Inserting a zip

Layering and clipping

Sewing band cuffs

Sewing collars

Using bias binding

Cutting out fabric pieces

Accurate and careful cutting is a key part of dressmaking. Getting this stage right will make later stages easier.

Pin the pattern piece to the fabric, pinning close to the edge of the pattern and ensuring that the paper lies as flat on the fabric as possible. If you use too many pins then the pattern piece may crinkle and cause problems later.

When cutting out, try not to lift the pattern and fabric too high, because this may result in you pulling the fabric and cutting it slightly smaller than the pattern piece. Rest the bottom blade of the scissors on the surface and cut in even, long cuts. Also, never cut out a fabric piece that includes the selvage because this will cause problems with the hang of the garment once it has been washed (see page 17).

Open Seam

This is a versatile basic seam and is suitable for most projects.

1 Place the fabric pieces right sides together and machine-sew 1.5cm (⅝ in) in from the edge.

2 Neaten the edges of the seam allowances using your preferred method – overlocker, zigzag stitch or pinking shears.

3 Press the seam allowances open for a neat finish.

Stay Stitching

Stay stitching should be done once the garment has been cut out, but before you start to make it up. It is done mainly on curved edges, such as necklines and armholes, to prevent the fabric from being pulled out of shape as you work.

To stay stitch, machine-sew through one layer of fabric 1cm (⅜ in) in from the edge, so that the stitching does not show on the outside of the garment when it is completed.

On a neckline, start at one shoulder point and sew around the curve. When you reach the midway point, stop sewing. Start again on the other shoulder point and sew around to the same position. Sewing in this way will mean you 'push' the fabric on both sides to the middle. If you were to stitch from one side right around the curve to the other side, then on one side you would be pushing the fabric into the middle and on the other side you would be pushing the fabric towards the shoulder. This would result in an uneven neckline once you have finished sewing. Do not knot the threads, instead clip them off close to the fabric.

stitching within the seam allowance

If you find it difficult to sew within the seam allowance, or if the fabric is very lightweight and tends to pucker when you sew so close to the edge, then cut the seam allowances wider, do the stay stitching, then trim the allowances down.

tailor's tacks

A tailor's tack is a way of marking the fabric while the pattern piece is still attached to it. This way, when the fabric is removed from the paper, important pattern markings, such as the tips of darts (see page 21), are not lost.

To make a tailor's tack, first thread a needle with a brightly coloured thread, one that will stand out against the colour of the fabric. Have the thread doubled, but do not knot the ends.

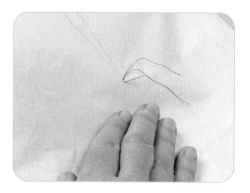

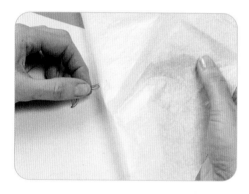

1 Push the needle through the paper pattern and the layers of fabric and pull the thread through, leaving about 5cm (2 in) of thread on the front. Push the needle back through the fabric in the same spot, creating a loop on the underside.

2 Push the needle through again, creating a loop of thread on the front of the fabric. Take the needle through to the back and cut the thread approximately 5cm (2 in) from the fabric.

3 Carefully lift the paper pattern piece off the fabric, holding the threads in place so that they are not pulled out.

4 Gently pull the pieces of fabric apart a little, then snip the threads of the tailor's tack in the middle.

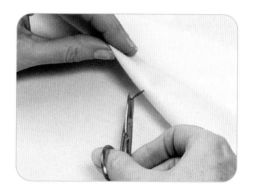

The point is now marked in such a way that, when the garment is finished, the threads can easily be pulled out leaving no trace.

sewing darts

Darts are used to add shaping to a garment and will usually appear on a bodice to enhance the bust, on skirts and trousers to enhance the waist and on sleeves to help the fit around the elbow. If sewn correctly they improve a garment, but if sewn incorrectly they can ruin an otherwise well-made project.

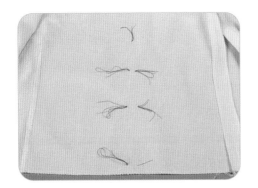

1 Ensure you have completed all the tailor's tacks (see page 20) required, as marked on your pattern piece.

2 Fold the fabric with the right sides together, matching the tailor's tacks carefully. Pin and tack the dart along the line of tacks.

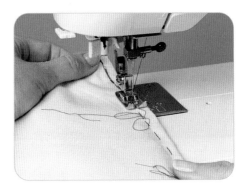

3 From the edge of the fabric, machine-sew along the line of tacking. At the point, finish sewing as near the edge as possible. Securely knot all threads.

4 Remove the tailor's tacks and tacking threads. Press the dart to one side. Press a bust dart down the body and press a vertical dart outwards to the side of the body.

making perfect darts

When marking a dart with tailor's tacks (see page 20), make tacks at the point, the open end (if it is a single-pointed dart), and the mid-way point.

If the dart is wider than 2cm (1 in) at the base, cut it open along the fold. The turnings should be pressed open and the edges neatened.

For instructions on how to move the position of a dart on a bodice, see Throwing A Dart, page 55.

Reverse-stitch three or four stitches at the point to secure the dart.

Setting in a fitted sleeve

The pattern created by draping the sleeve (see pages 42–45) will be slightly larger around the sleeve head than the armhole is in the bodice. Therefore the sleeve must be eased into place, which also gives a lovely tailored look and adds ease of movement to the garment without the use of darts or gathers.

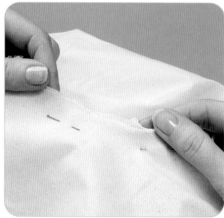

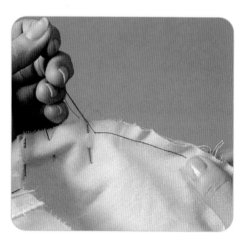

1 Loosen the stitch tension on the machine slightly, then sew a line of stitching inside the seam allowance, sewing across the top of the sleeve head between the underarm section on the front and the underarm section on the back of the sleeve. Turn the sleeve right-side out and insert it into the armhole. Match the underarm seam on the sleeve and the side seam on the bodice and pin the pieces together at that point.

2 Pin the underarm section in place, matching up the edges of the fabric to the point where you meet the line of stitching sewn in Step 1.

change your tension!

Before you sew the sleeve in place remember to re-tighten the tension on your machine because you loosened it in Step 1.

3 Match the shoulder point on the sleeve head to the shoulder line. Then carefully pull on the threads of the line of stitching to gather up the sleeve head until it fits into the armhole.

Working from the middle outwards to each side, pin the sleeve in place, ensuring that the gathers are evenly spaced. The gathers should be small enough so that when the garment is completed they do not show on the outside. Tack the sleeve in place and then machine-sew the seam. Remove the gathering and tacking threads.

Setting in a gathered sleeve

A few of the sleeve patterns in this book (see pages 82–89) require a sleeve with a gathered head. Once you have cut the fabric piece, follow these steps to create neat, even gathers. The technique can easily be adapted and used to gather other pattern pieces, such as the bust section on tops and dresses.

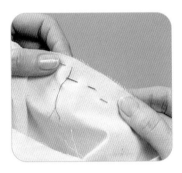

1 Using a brightly coloured thread and short stitches, sew a line of gathering stitches between the two marks on the pattern (see page 54).

2 Fit the sleeve into the armhole. Match the underarm seam and side seam and pin to the start of the gathering stitches. Match the shoulder point on the sleeve and the shoulder seam of the bodice and pin.

3 Now gently pull on the thread of the gathering stitches until the sleeve head is the same size as the armhole.

4 Once the sleeve head is the same size as the armhole, fasten off the threads by wrapping them in a figure of eight around a pin.

5 Tack and then machine-sew the sleeve. Remove the gathering/tacking threads.

gathering fabric

When gathering long sections, divide both pieces of fabric into four equal parts. You can then gather and fit one section at a time, making it easier to ensure that the gathers are evenly spaced.

Always use short, tight tacking stitches to hold the gathering in place while machine-sewing. Loose stitches can allow the pressure of the machine foot to push the fabric into bunches, which ruin the evenness of your gathers.

inserting a Zip

There are a number of methods for inserting a zip; some are more suitable for trousers, while others are more suitable for skirts and dresses. The method shown here is suitable for most occasions and is perhaps the easiest method to learn if you have never put in a zip before.

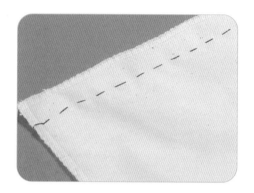

1 Sew the seam in the usual way, finishing at the point where the end of the zip will be. Neaten the edges of the fabric then tack the zip opening closed, following the line of the seam. Press the seam, including the zip section, open.

2 Place the zip so that the teeth are directly over the tacked seam and the top of the zip tape is aligned with the top of the fabric. If you align the zip pull with the top of the fabric, you will not be able to attach a facing or waistband.

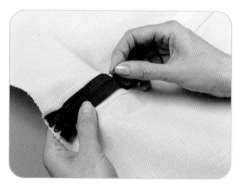

3 Pin the zip in position then tack it. Use a brightly coloured thread and small, tight hand stitches to hold the zip securely.

4 Using a zip foot on your sewing machine, start at the top and sew down one side of the zip, sewing as close to the teeth as possible. Pivot at the bottom of the zip and sew across the tape three or four times. Knot the threads securely then cut them. Starting at the top again, sew down the other side of the zip, then knot and cut the threads. Sewing from the top down on both sides avoids pulling the fabric in different directions.

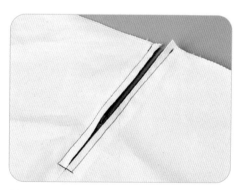

The zip is hidden once it is done up, but the sewing lines are visible so ensure that the top and bottom threads match the fabric.

inserting zips

- Try to match the zip length to the size of the opening (most shop-bought patterns will give the length of zip required).

- Ensure that your garment fits you properly before inserting the zip.

- Match the zip colour as closely as possible to the fabric colour. Zips come in a fairly limited range of colours, so it's unlikely that you'll get a perfect match. Choose one that is a darker shade rather than a lighter shade because this will show less.

- Try to match the zip type to the garment fabric. Use nylon-toothed zips with lightweight fabrics and metal-toothed zips with heavyweight fabrics.

- Before inserting a zip, check that it runs smoothly: you do not want the frustration of having sewn in a faulty zip and then having to remove it.

- When pinning a zip into place, pin it from the bottom up.

- When sewing on a machine, always use a zip foot.

layering and clipping

For a professional finish to your sewing it is always advisable to try and reduce bulk on seams, especially on collars and cuffs or when using heavyweight fabrics. This is easily done using the techniques called layering and clipping.

Layering

This is used to reduce the bulk of a seam before you turn a collar or cuff right-side out. Using small, sharp scissors, trim the seam allowance down by about half its width. This is best done on the layer of fabric that has been interfaced. If you are trimming fabric that has not been interfaced and are worried it may fray, you can trim with pinking shears.

Clipping

Before you turn a collar or cuff, clip excess fabric off corners. Using small, sharp scissors, cut across the corner just outside the line of stitching.

You should also clip into curves such as necklines, snipping from the outside edge up to the seam, (without cutting the seam stitches) every 2.5cm (1 in) to allow the fabric to lie flat.

sewing band cuffs

Creating a well-fitted, neatly sewn cuff can make or break any sleeve and, with a little attention to detail, it is easier than you might think.

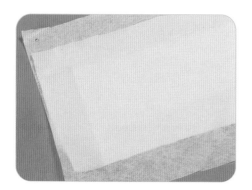

1 Before you start to sew you will need to cut out the fabric pieces, plus a suitable interfacing (see page 16) for each cuff.

2 Attach the interfacing to the wrong side of the fabric then press any fold lines marked on the pattern. With right sides together, sew the ends of the cuff together to create a circle of fabric. With right sides together, pin one edge of the band cuff to the end of the sleeve, matching the raw edges of the fabric. Tack the layers of fabric together.

3 Remove the flat bed from your sewing machine and sew the cuff to the sleeve, taking the suggested seam allowance; this is usually 1.5cm (⅝ in).

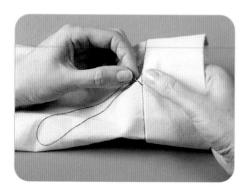

4 Fold the cuff out flat and press the seam towards it. Turn the sleeve and cuff inside out. Fold the cuff back on itself along the middle fold line and fold under the seam allowance. Using slip stitch, sew the inside of the cuff in place, sewing just inside the line of machine stitching attaching the cuff to the sleeve.

Using this method you will make a neat cuff with all raw edges encased and the hand stitching will not be seen on the right side of the garment

layering and clipping

For a truly professional finish to your cuffs, remember to layer seams and clip corners (see page 25).

Sewing Collars

Collars hold the same horror for many home sewers as cuffs do. However, if you've mastered the technique of fitting a band cuff, then a collar is just as easy. It's merely a question of good sewing practices.

This method makes a collar that is fitted to a garment and does not have a lining or facing. It ensures that all raw edges are hidden once it is completed.

making great collars

Attach the interfacing to the section that will be the underside of the collar.

When using heavier-weight fabrics, trim the interfacing very close to the line of stitching to reduce bulk.

If the fabric is heavyweight or does not have a lot of give, then make the upper collar section just a little wider than the underside section to help the collar to sit comfortably.

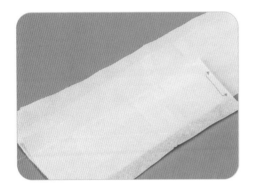

1 When cutting out the collar, cut the two fabric pieces and one layer from suitable interfacing (see page 16).

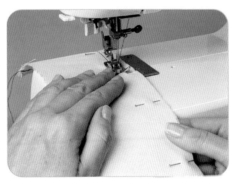

2 Attach the interfacing to the wrong side of one piece of fabric. With right sides together, sew around the three outer edges of the collar. The edge to be attached to the garment should be left open.

3 Layer the seams and clip the corners (see page 25) to reduce bulk and to give a good finish to the collar. Turn it right side out and press it well.

4 Line up the centre back point of the collar with the centre back of the bodice, then pin and tack it in place. Machine-sew the collar to the bodice then fold under the seam allowance on the inside section. Using slip stitch, sew the inside of the collar in place as for a cuff (see page 26).

using bias binding

Bias binding is a great solution for finishing off plain armholes and necklines, and it can also be used to finish seams and even neaten hems. If you do not mind a line of stitching being visible on the outside of the garment, then you can use your sewing machine from start to finish. However, if you want to have as little sewing as possible showing on the outside of your garment, use the hand-finishing method. The hand-finishing method can also make it easier to achieve a neat finish if you are binding a curved edge.

Machine-sewing method of attaching bias binding

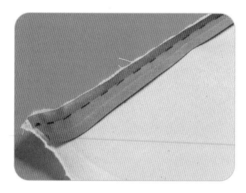

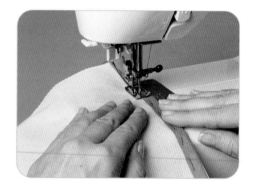

1 Open out one side of the bias binding and pin it to the right side of the fabric so that the opened fold in the binding lies on the stitching line. Note that the seam allowance cannot be wider than the folded bias binding. Tack the bias binding in place.

2 Machine-sew along the fold line in the binding, following it as accurately as possible.

3 Press the bias binding to the wrong side of the fabric and pin or tack it in place. Machine-sew a second line of stitching close to the free edge of the bias binding.

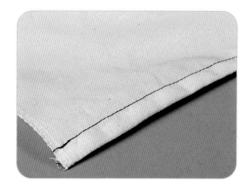

This method will result in a line of stitching showing on the right side of the fabric. For clarity we have sewn with black thread, but you can obviously lessen the impact of this stitching by using a thread that matches the colour of the fabric.

Hand-sewing method of attaching bias binding

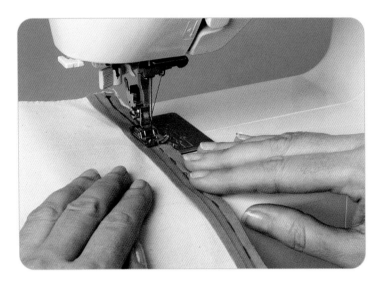

△ 1 Open out one side of the bias binding and pin it to the right side of the fabric so that the opened fold in the binding lies on the stitching line. Note that the seam allowance cannot be wider than the folded bias binding. Tack then machine-sew along the fold line.

△ 2 Press the bias binding to the wrong side of the fabric and pin it in place. Using slip stitch, sew the free edge of the binding to the fabric.

better bias binding

You can use bias binding as a decorative trimming by sewing it on so that it is on the right side of the fabric.

Between each step give the bias binding a good press, this will help it sit better.

You can make your own bias binding with the aid of this neat little bias binding device that is available from many good sewing shops. Simply cut fabric strips on the true bias (at 45 degrees to the selvage) to the correct width (the binding makers come in different sizes to make different widths of binding). Then feed the strips through the device and press the folds.

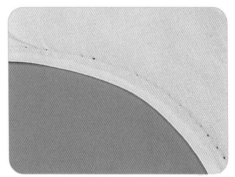

Again, we have used black thread for clarity, but a matching thread would result in stitches that are almost invisible on the right side of the fabric.

draping your basic blocks

This section covers the techniques for draping calico directly onto the body to create a garment block. You'll need a family member or a friend to help you with these easy processes that will allow you to create garments that fit perfectly.

Basic front bodice

Basic back bodice

Basic fitted sleeve

Basic skirt

the principles of draping

Draping fabric on the body is a traditional technique used by couturiers and dressmakers for centuries. For making garment blocks, it's quicker, simpler and just as accurate as the mathematical method of measuring, calculating and plotting on paper. Once you have completed the draping process, the calico block is turned into a paper block that can then be used to create patterns.

Choosing fabric

Inexpensive lightweight calico is the best fabric to use. It is fairly close-woven so it will not stretch while you are draping, yet it is not so fine that the warp and weft threads (see below) are difficult to find. You can use plain cotton if you have some in your fabric stash, but do not use anything that is stretchy or slippery.

Finding straight of grain

Before you start draping you need to cut and prepare the calico. This involves finding the straight of grain so that you can cut the calico accurately.

All woven fabrics have what are called the warp and weft threads and these are the grain of the fabric. The warp threads are the threads that run the length of the fabric and the weft threads are those that run from selvage to selvage (edge to edge).

The warp threads run parallel to the selvage (which is tighter than the main fabric), and tend to be stronger than the weft threads. To follow the straight of grain, the cut edge of the fabric must be true to the warp or weft.

To find the warp, cut off the selvage then pull out threads until you are able to pull out one continuous thread the length of the cut piece. To find the weft, cut across the fabric then pull out threads in the same way. Trim off any protruding ends of threads.

Tacking

The pieces of calico need to be marked with lines of tacking stitches. Work these in a brightly coloured thread so that you can see them easily.

Fold the calico on the straight of grain where you need the line to be and iron it. Tack along this crease making small, neat stitches. The lines of tacking must run parallel to the edges of the calico.

If you prefer, you can draw lines on the calico using a long rule and fine-tip, bright-coloured permanent marker.

Ease darts

A garment block cannot be skin-tight or you will not be able to move freely. The best way to allow for this is to pin small darts into the calico before draping it; these are the 'ease darts'.

Each block gives instructions for where to pin the ease dart and how wide it should be. For a 6mm (¼ in) dart, you need to measure out 12mm (½ in) of fabric and then fold this in half and pin it.

What to wear

For draping the bodice and sleeve, wear a tight-fitting top, such as a thin T-shirt; long sleeves can be useful for ease of pinning. The top needs to be arranged on the body with all the seams in the right places.

When pinning the calico to it, be careful not to drag the seams out of position as you are partly relying on these as guides for your block. Wear a good bra to ensure you make the best of what you have.

For draping the skirt, a pair of tight-fitting jeans or leggings is best. As with the top, ensure that seams are in the right places and do not pull them out of place when pinning.

Which side to drape

For a figure that is symmetrical, you can use a single layer of fabric to drape on the right-hand side of the body.

However, if the left-hand side is a little larger, then drape on that side. If there is a big difference between the left- and right-hand sides of the body, then drape both sides.

Pinning the block

As you will be working directly onto the body of a family member or friend, you MUST take care with the pins. Always lift the garment being worn and the calico block you are working on slightly away from the body before putting in a pin. Hold the pin at an angle of no more than 30 degrees; this should reduce the risk of sticking the pin in the person being draped upon.

Dresses and trousers

A dress block is made by combining the basic bodice and skirt blocks (see page 58).

Draping trousers is difficult, so to allow you to create a trouser block we have included an easier method that involves altering the skirt block directly onto paper (see page 60).

Checking the blocks

Before using a block to draft your own patterns create a toile to ensure darts, seams and ease are correct. To do this, use the paper blocks you have made (see pages 52–63) to cut calico pieces, remembering to add seam allowances where needed.

Make these pieces up on the sewing machine, though there is no need for refinements such as finishing seams or hemming.

Try this toile on and move around in it to ensure it is comfortable. Make any adjustments needed and re-draw the paper pattern if required.

for the draping process you will need:

- A friend to help you
- A tight-fitting top and trousers
- Lightweight calico (the amount depends on body size)
- Plenty of good-quality pins
- Fabric marker or pencil (see page 12)
- Tape measure
- Hand-sewing needle
- Brightly coloured thread
- Fabric scissors
- Small pair of sharp scissors

friend indeed

Make the draping fun by getting together with a sewing friend and draping one another. You both get blocks and have a good day.

the basic bodice front

The basic bodice is the starting point for all tops and dresses, so it's important that it fits you perfectly. Draping the bodice is carried out in two halves, first the front, then the back. Most people will be able to drape just the right-hand side of their body (see page 33), as shown here.

cutting the calico

1 Measure the length of the front body from the highest shoulder point to the natural waistline and across the widest part of the body (see pages 10–11). Add 15cm (6 in) to these measurements to allow for manipulation in both directions and cut the calico to size, making sure the edges follow the straight of grain (see page 32).

2 Measure from the shoulder line at the neck down to just below the underarm. Add 7.5cm (3 in) to this measurement and mark this underarm line right across the calico with a line of tacking stitches, ensuring you follow the weft threads of the calico.

3 Measure in 5cm (2 in) in from the right-hand edge and mark this centre front line right down the calico with a line of tacking stitches, ensuring you follow the warp threads of the calico.

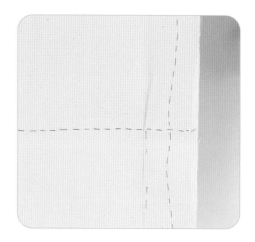

▲ 1 Along the lower edge, between 5cm (2 in) and 10cm (4 in) in from the centre front line, create an ease dart (see page 32) 6mm (¼ in) wide. The dart should lie between the centre front and the bust point (this may need to be checked on the body). Extend the dart up to end level with the underarm line. If you prefer a little more ease, then make the dart 13mm (½ in) wide.

before you start

Make sure that the room is warm enough for the person being draped upon as they are going to have to stand still for a while wearing only a thin T-shirt. Make sure your small fabric scissors, fabric marker or pencil and pins are to hand.

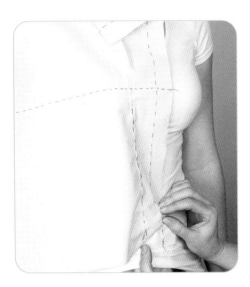

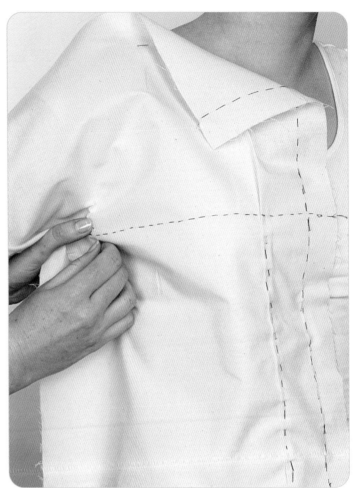

2 Begin by pinning the centre front line to the centre front line of the body, ensuring the horizontal line of tacking stitches is just below the underarm.

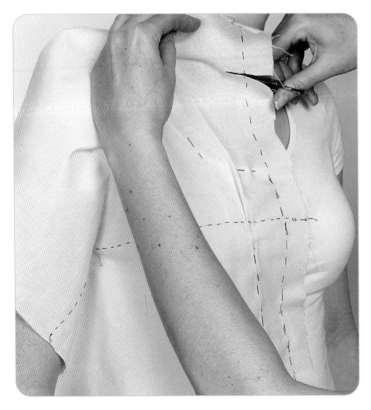

3 Smooth the calico across the body, keeping the underarm line horizontal, and pin it under the arm to the side seam of the T-shirt being worn.

4 Smooth the calico around the neck, pinning it to the neckline of the T-shirt. Carefully cut away the square corner of the calico, cutting in a smooth curve around the base of the neck. Snip the calico down to the neckline if you find that it does not lie flat against the body.

continued next page ➤ ➤ ➤

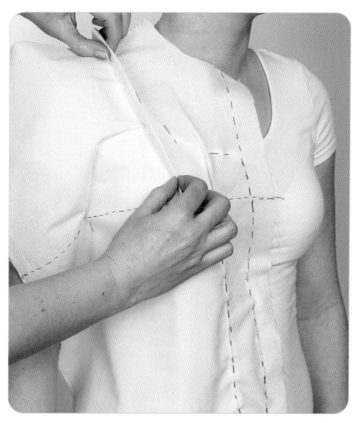

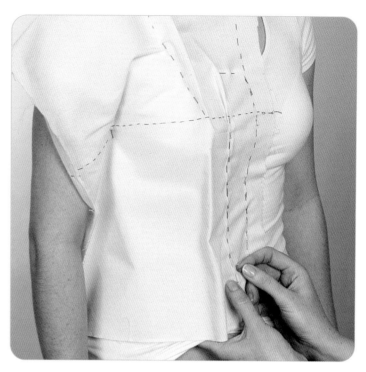

6 Smooth the calico from the centre front along the waistline, pinning as you work, to the point directly beneath the bust point.

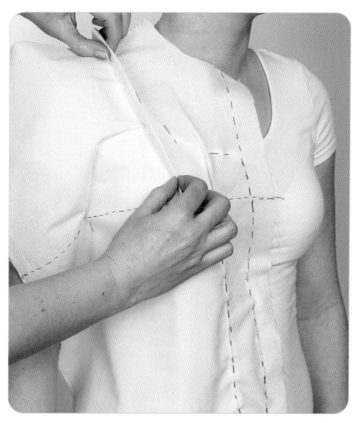
5 Measure the shoulder length and pin halfway along this line from the highest neck point. Ensure that the shoulder line runs along the centre of the shoulder to the shoulder point (use the T-shirt shoulder seam as a guide). Take in the excess fabric by folding it into a dart that runs down to just above the widest point of the bust. Pin the dart in place.

7 Ensuring that the edge of the calico hangs vertically, pin the side seam in place down to the waistline, pinning the calico to the T-shirt side seam. If you wish, trim off fabric beyond the pinned side seam, leaving just 5cm (2 in) excess.

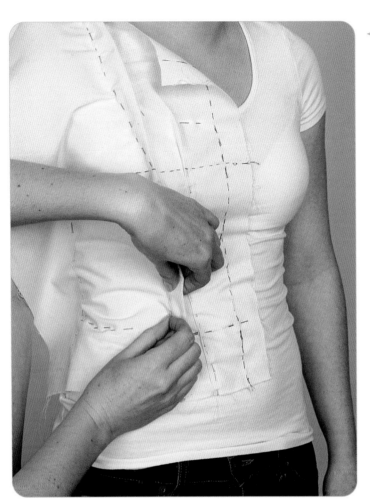

8 Now smooth the calico from the side seam along the waistline to the point already pinned in Step 6. Pin excess calico into a dart that travels vertically straight up the body, ending just short of the bust point.

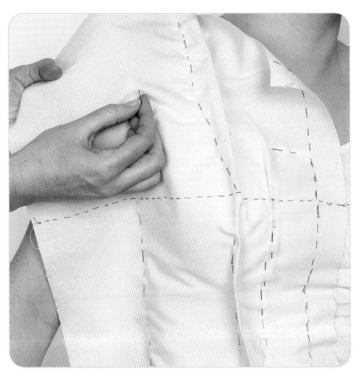

9 Pinning as you work, smooth the calico from the pinned underarm point around the armhole, then up to the shoulder point. If you wish, trim off excess calico around the armhole, then snip into it if necessary so that it lies flat.

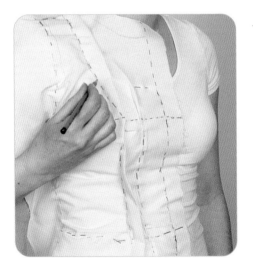

10 Using a fabric marker or pencil (see page 12) and following the lines of pins, draw in the side seam, waist seam, down either side of both darts and around the armhole and neck. Check that the seams on the T-shirt are all sitting in the right places before drawing in the lines.

the basic bodice back

Leave the front bodice pinned to the T-shirt while draping the back bodice. If the excess front bodice fabric makes draping the back bodice tricky, then trim it away leaving at least 5cm (2 in) of fabric outside the pencil lines.

cutting the calico

1 Measure the length of the back body from the highest shoulder point to the natural waistline and across the widest part of the body. Add 15cm (6 in) to these measurements to allow for manipulation in both directions and cut the calico to size, making sure the edges follow the straight of grain (see page 32).

2 Measure from the shoulder line at the neck down to just below the underarm. Add 7.5cm (3 in) to this measurement and mark this underarm line right across the calico with a line of tacking stitches, ensuring you follow the weft threads of the calico.

3 Measure in 5cm (2 in) in from the right-hand edge and mark this centre back line right down the calico with a line of tacking stitches, ensuring you follow the warp threads of the calico.

4 Along the lower edge, between 5cm (2 in) and 10cm (4 in) in from the centre back line, create an ease dart (see page 32) 6mm (¼ in) wide. The dart should lie between the centre front and the middle of the shoulder blades (this may need to be checked on the body). Extend the dart up to end level with the underarm line. If you prefer a little more ease, then make the dart 13mm (½ in) wide.

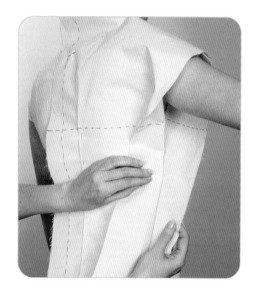

▲1 Pin the centre back line in place at the neck point, lining up the tacked underarm line on the back bodice with the tacked underarm line on the front bodice.

long hair

If the person being draped upon has long hair, ask them to pin it up out of the way to avoid an accidental haircut when you trim the calico.

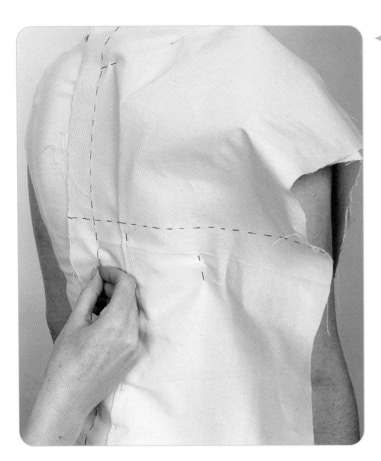

2 Pin the calico to the T-shirt up the centre back, ensuring that the tacked line stays vertical.

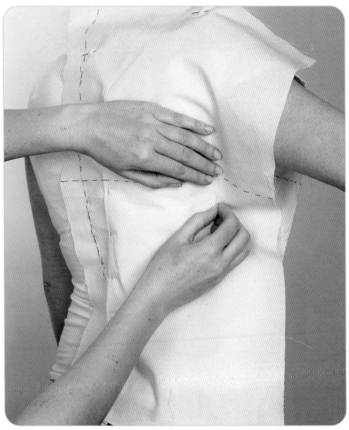

3 Smooth the calico across the body, keeping the underarm line horizontal, and pin it under the arm, making sure that the tacked underarm line aligns with the same line on the bodice front.

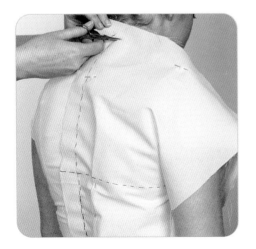

4 Smooth the calico around the neckline, pinning as you go. If necessary, trim the calico down to the neckline to ensure that it lies flat against the body.

continued next page ➤ ➤ ➤

the basic bodice back

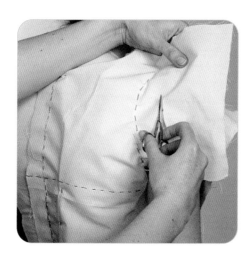

5 Working upwards from the underarm, smooth the calico around the armhole, pinning it as you work up to the shoulder point. Cut away excess fabric around the armhole and snip into it if required.

6 There will be a little extra fabric along the shoulder line and this is folded into a dart. This dart should be placed halfway along the shoulder line and run parallel to the centre back line. It should be between 7.5cm (3 in) and 10cm (4 in) in length, depending on body shape and size.

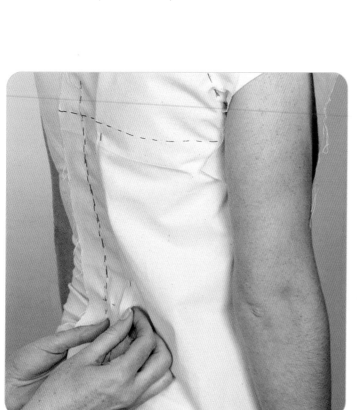

7 Smooth out the calico from the centre back line, pinning along the waistline to the point directly below the centre of the shoulder blades.

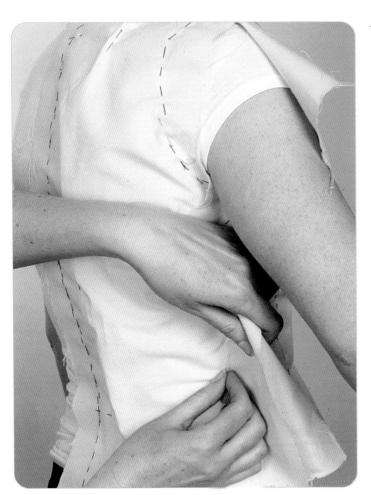

8 Ensure that the edge of the calico is hanging vertically and pin the side seam in place down to the waistline. Trim the excess fabric beyond the side seam (using the edge of the front bodice as a guide) if you need to reduce the amount of fabric.

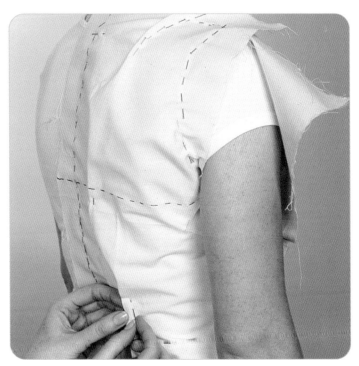

9 Smooth the calico along the waist from the side seam to the point already pinned. Pin the excess fabric into a dart that travels vertically straight up the body to the centre of the shoulder blades.

10 Draw in the waistline, waist dart, side seam, armhole, shoulder line, shoulder dart and neckline in the same way as for the front bodice (see page 37).

the basic fitted sleeve

Once you have draped the bodice, you need to drape a sleeve. Leave the bodice pinned to the body while doing this.

cutting the calico

1. Measure around the armhole on the bodice and from the shoulder point to the wrist length (usually the prominent bone at the wrist). Add 20cm (8 in) to both of these measurements and cut a piece of calico to size, making sure the edges follow the straight of grain (see page 32).

2. Fold the calico in half lengthwise and crease it. Work a line of tacking stitches along the crease, ensuring you follow the straight of the grain.

3. Measure down from the shoulder point to the widest part of the bicep. Add 10cm (4 in) to this measurement and mark a cross line right across the calico with a line of tacking stitches, ensuring you follow the straight of grain.

4. Fold a 1cm (³⁄₈ in) ease dart right along the centre line

1. Match the tacked centre line on the sleeve to the shoulder line (the seam between the two halves of the bodice), lining up the cross line with the widest part of the upper arm. Put in a pin at the top of the sleeve.

long sleeves

A long-sleeved T-shirt can make pinning the draped sleeve a little easier, but the T-shirt sleeves do need to fit very tightly. Otherwise wear a short-sleeved top, it won't be a problem.

2 With the arm held away from the body, smooth the calico around the arm and match the ends of the cross line under the arm. Put a pin through the cross line, making sure the sleeve is not too tight and that the centre line runs down the centre of the upper arm.

3 Pin the sleeve up to the underarm, keeping the centre line straight and ensuring that when the arm hangs down by the body, the underarm seam follows the side seam of the bodice.

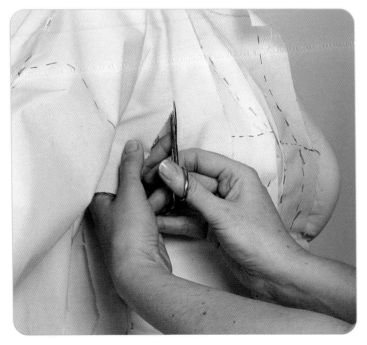

4 Smooth the calico around the front armhole, following the armhole of the bodice and pinning the sleeve to the bodice armhole along the line of pins that holds the bodice armhole to the T-shirt. If necessary, trim off excess fabric, leaving 2.5cm (1 in) of fabric beyond the pins.

continued next page ➤ ➤ ➤

the basic fitted sleeve 43

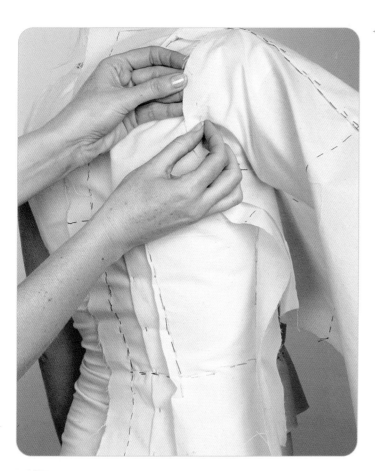

5 Repeat this process for the back of the armhole, again following the line of pins on the bodice armhole and trimming fabric as needed.

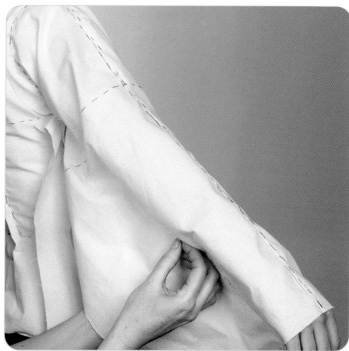

6 Smooth the calico around the lower section of the arm and pin the underarm down to the wrist. Ensure that the centre line is straight and that, when the arm hangs down by the body, the underarm seam follows the side seam of the bodice.

7 With the arm held out and slightly bent, create a small elbow dart parallel to the cross line. The dart should be 13mm (½ in) at its widest point, tapering to nothing at the point of the elbow.

8 With the elbow bent, mark the wrist line. This is usually level with the small bone on the outer wrist.

9 With a fabric marker or pencil (see page 12) and following the lines of pins, draw in the armhole curve, the dart, the wrist line, and the underarm seam.

the perfect sleeve

Before using this block for a garment, make a calico sleeve from it and attach to a made-up bodice. Then check to ensure that the sleeve fits correctly by moving your arm in all directions. Alter the sleeve as necessary to ensure a comfortable fit.

If you do not adapt this sleeve block to introduce gathering or pleats in the head then it will need to be eased in to the bodice armhole to create a fitted sleeve (see page 22).

the basic skirt

Once you have mastered the techniques of draping the bodice and the sleeve, then draping a skirt is very easy and opens up so many possibilities – from skirts to dresses and trousers. If you are not draping the bodice in the same session, then the wearer will need to wear a made-up calico bodice.

cutting the calico

1 Measure from the natural waistline to just below knee level: this skirt length is used for ease of draping, but the length can be altered once the calico block has been converted into a paper block. Work out half the front width and half the back width across the hips (see page 10).

2 Add 20cm (8 in) to both these measurements and cut two pieces of calico, one for the front and one for the back of the skirt, making sure the edges follow the straight of grain.

3 Take one piece of calico (to be the front) and along one long edge, measure in 2.5cm (1 in). Mark this centre front line right down the calico with a line of tacking stitches, following the straight of grain.

4 Measure down from the waist to the widest point of the hips and add 10cm (4 in) to this measurement. Mark this hip line across the calico with a line of tacking stitches, following the straight of grain.

5 To create ease, fold in a dart from the lower edge (the hem line) up to just above the hip line. The dart should be 6mm (¼ in) deep and between 7.5cm (3 in) and 12.5cm (5 in) in from the centre front line, lying between the centre front line and the bust point on the front bodice.

6 Measure across the hip line from the tacked centre front line to half the hip width and mark this side seam with a line of tacking stitches down to the hem. Repeat Steps 1–6 on the second piece of calico for the back of the skirt, making a 1cm (⅜ in) ease dart, as before.

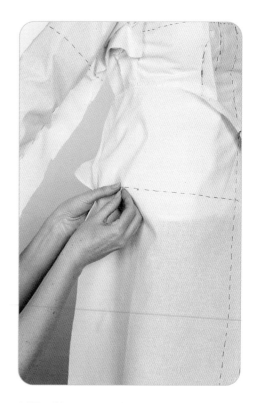

▲1 Hang the skirt on the right-hand side of the body and pin the calico 5cm (2 in) to 10cm (4 in) above the waistline. Ensure that the centre front line hangs vertically and the tacked hip line is on the widest part of the hip. Put in a pin on the hip line.

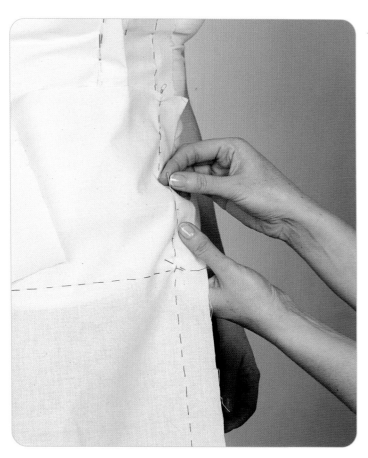

2 Pin down the centre front as far as you can, this may only be to the hip level if your model is wearing trousers.

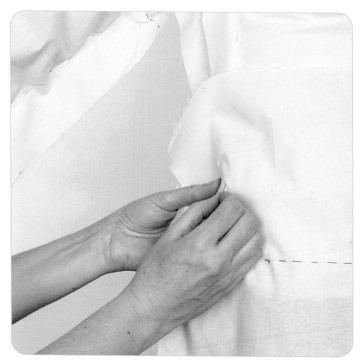

3 Ensuring that the hip line is horizontal, smooth up from the hip point to the waistline and pin. (The fabric will curve out around the waist and this will be dealt with in later steps.)

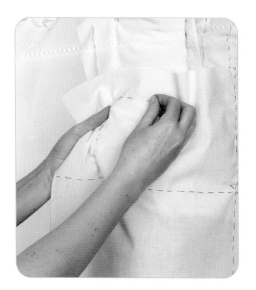

4 Smooth the calico across the waistline from the side seam, pinning as you work, until you reach the position of the bust dart on the front bodice.

continued next page ➤ ➤ ➤

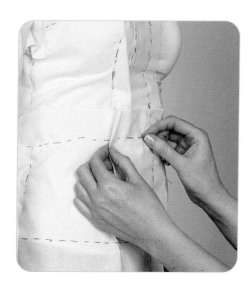

5 Smooth the calico across the waistline from the centre front line, pinning as you work, until you reach the position of the bust dart on the front bodice.

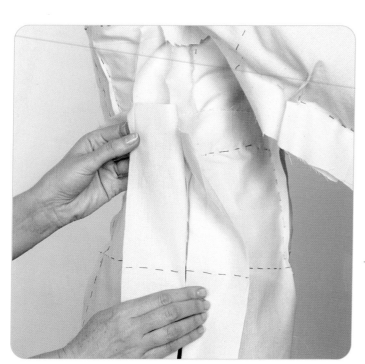

6 Fold the excess fabric at the waist to make the waist dart, ensuring that this is parallel to the tacked centre front line. You may find you have to adjust the pinning of the side seam at the waist to ensure a comfortable fit.

7 Pin the back skirt piece of calico in place as for the front skirt piece (see Step 1), ensuring that the hip lines match at the side seam.

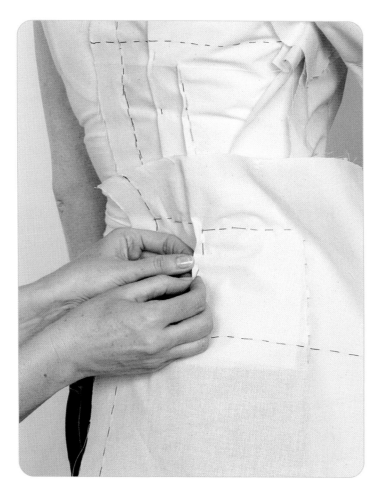

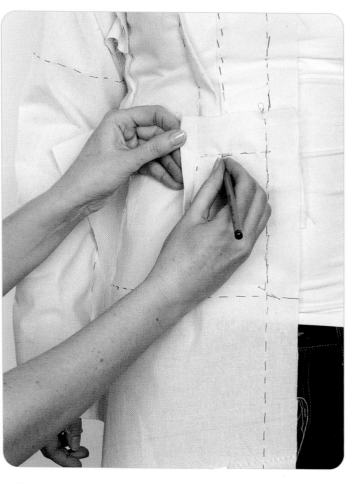

▲8 Pin up the centre back, up the side seam, and across from the centre back and then the side seam to the dart position, as you did for the front skirt. Pin the dart in place.

▲9 Using a fabric marker or pencil (see page 12) and following the pinned lines, draw in side seam, waistline, centre lines and darts on both of the skirt pieces.

be honest

Don't suck in your tummy when having the skirt block draped: the whole point is to make a block that fits perfectly. If you're worried about a round tummy, then make the flared skirt pattern (see page 92), which skims the tummy flatteringly.

making your paper blocks

Now that you have draped the calico to create fabric blocks, you need to turn these into working paper blocks. Once these are made, you can create a dress block from your bodice and skirt blocks and a trouser block from your skirt block. You can then use these paper blocks to create any of the patterns we have in this book (see pages 64–113), as well as other patterns you design yourself.

Turning your calicos into paper blocks

Adding pattern markings

Throwing a dart

Sample patterns

Making a dress block

Making a loose sleeve block

Making a trouser block

turning your calicos into paper blocks

Draping the calico was the trickiest part of the process of creating personalised pattern blocks. Now that you have done that, you are ready to undertake the easy part – making the paper blocks. The process is shown here on the bodice front block, but is exactly the same for the bodice back, sleeve and skirt blocks.

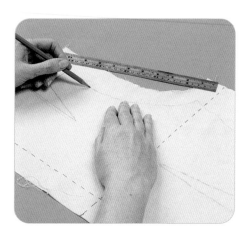

1 Press the calico to ensure it lies flat on your work surface. Using the pencil, draw over all the drawn lines to darken them. Use the rule to straighten any wobbly lines and flexible curve rule (if you wish) to neaten any curved lines.

2 Ensure that the darts are positioned correctly (see Positioning Darts, opposite). On the bodice and skirt blocks, the waistline and centre lines must be at 90 degrees to one another.

3 Lay the drafting paper over the calico block and trace all the lines. Be very accurate as this is the pattern block you will use to make up garments.

4 Insert balance marks where needed; for example, on the armhole curve of the bodice. Measure down 5cm (2 in) from shoulder line. Then, on the front bodice draw one triangle with the point on the 5cm (2 in) mark and on the back bodice draw one triangle either side of the 5cm (2 in) mark.

On the sleeve head, mark in the centre line; this will line up with the shoulder seams on the bodice. Then draw balance marks to match those on the front and back bodice armholes, measuring 5cm (2 in) out from the centre line around the curve of the sleeve head.

On the skirt, mark the hip line with a triangle on the front and back blocks.

For a full description of all pattern markings, turn to page 54.

positioning darts

The centre line of a shoulder dart should run at right angles to the shoulder line.

The centre line of the waist darts on bodices should run parallel to the centre front and back lines and the tips of the darts should fall just short of bust and shoulder blades.

The centre line on waistline of skirts and trousers should run parallel to the centre front and centre back lines.

If a dart is not correctly positioned, alter it now. Draw a light pencil line down the middle of the dart so that you can see the centre line clearly. For a shoulder dart, lay the set square on the shoulder line and re-draw the dart centre line at right angles. For waist darts, on the bodice and skirt, measure out from the tacked centre line to the bottom of the drawn dart centre line. Measure out the same distance at the top of the dart and re-draw the centre line from measured point to measured point. Then draw in the new dart lines sloping out from the tips of the darts.

Seam and hem allowances

Some people like to add the standard 1.5cm (⅝ in) seam allowances and 5cm (2 in) hems to a block before they start to use it for drafting patterns. However, others prefer to add these later. For the sake of clarity, all blocks and patterns in this book are shown without seam allowances. Therefore, when you are drafting your patterns, you must add seam allowances and hems once you have completed the drafting process.

Card blocks

If you are going to use your paper blocks time and time again, then it is advisable to turn them into blocks made of thin card. The easiest method is to lay a sheet of carbon paper between the card and the paper block and trace over the lines on the paper block. Then re-draw all the lines and all pattern markings with a fine black pen and cut out the blocks. To make transferring darts easier, cut a small 'V' at the ends of the two outside lines of the dart and make a small hole at the tip.

adding pattern markings

Once you have made your paper blocks you need to add relevant pattern markings. These give instructions for laying out the pieces on the fabric and help in the construction of the garment. Sometimes markings will alter when you turn blocks into patterns; for example, on the Top With Ruched Centre Front (see page 74) the centre front line becomes a seam so the 'place on fold' instruction is removed.

The basic abbreviations and reference letters used in pattern drafting are:

CB	*Centre Back*	WP	*Waist Point*
CF	*Centre Front*	B	*Bust*
NP	*Neck Point*	H	*Hips*
SP	*Shoulder Point*	W	*Waist*
HP	*Hip Point*	KL	*Knee Line*

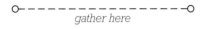
gather here

Gathering line
A broken line with a dot at either end with the wording 'gather here'. This pattern mark can also be used to indicate where a garment should be eased; in this instance the wording is 'ease here'.

Fold line
Represented by a line with right-angled arrows at either end that point to the edge that must be placed as close to the fold as possible.

Balance marks
Single, double or triple triangles on the outer edge of pattern pieces make it easier to match them up correctly.

Darts
These are shown as broken lines that meet at a point. A single dart is a 'V' shape and a double dart is a diamond shape. To make it easier to sew the dart later (see page 21), place two dots opposite each other halfway along the dart and one at the end, as shown.

Dots
These are placed where a seam line should start and or finish. Useful for fitting collars, etc., when it is important to finish or start the seam in the correct place. Dots are also placed at the end of an opening to indicate the position of a zip, sometimes with the word 'zip' inserted.

Buttonhole position
A line with two smaller lines coming from it, or two dots joined by a line.

Pleat
Two dashed or dotted lines with dots at the end running down from the edge of the pattern, with an arrow pointing in the direction the pleat should be made.

Grain line
This is a line with arrows at either end. It indicates in which direction the straight of grain should run.

throwing a dart

In some of the designs shown on pages 64–113 the basic shoulder dart has to be moved to another position on the bodice; this is known as 'throwing the dart'. It is a simple process that allows you to change the shape of the bodice.

1 Overlay your basic bodice block with a sheet of drafting paper and trace it.

2 Mark the new position of the dart, ensuring that its point touches the point of the dart being removed.

shaping darts

Although most darts are drawn with straight sides, slightly curving the sides inwards or outwards can be beneficial. For example, if the person has a larger than average bust and a small waist, sometimes curving the side of the darts outwards slightly gives a better fit.

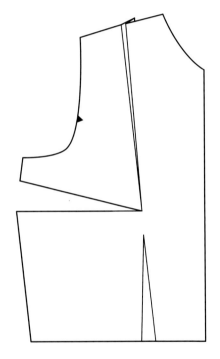

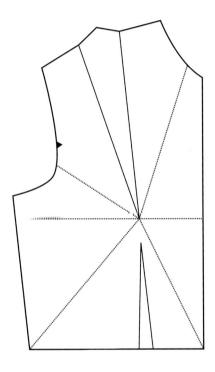

3 Cut along the line of the new dart. Fold out the unwanted dart and the pattern will open up to make a new dart where you have cut the paper.

4 Retrace the pattern, drawing in the new dart position.

The diagram shows the standard dart positions, but you can place the dart wherever you wish.

Sample patterns

These diagrams show how your finished blocks should appear. However, remember that as everyone is a different shape, your blocks may look slightly different to these.

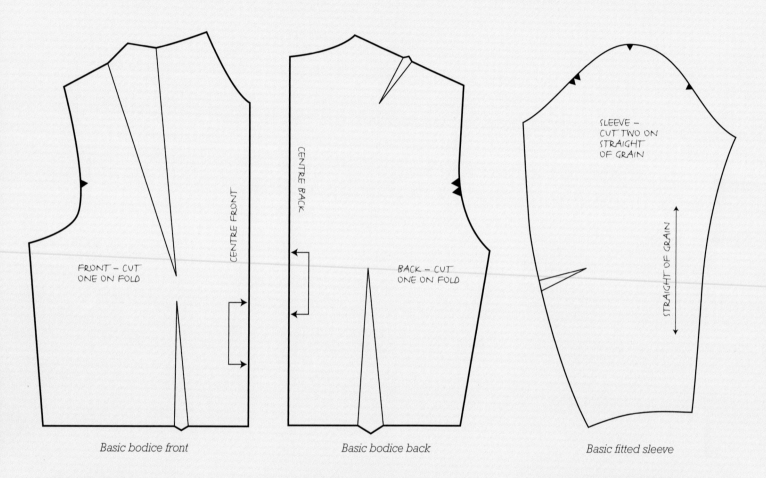

Basic bodice front

Basic bodice back

Basic fitted sleeve

dart points

To ensure that the edge of the fabric does not dip, you will need to add a small point to most dart ends. To do this, fold the dart on the pattern then trace over the section of the seam where the dart is folded with a pencil. Then unfold the dart and draw in the resulting point.

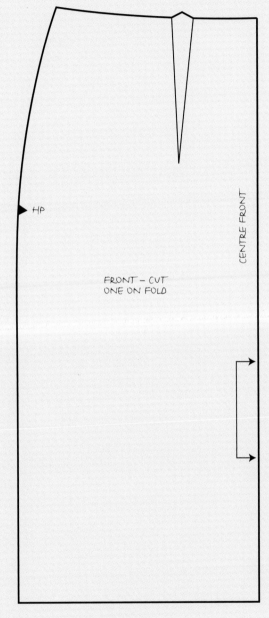

HP

CENTRE FRONT

FRONT – CUT
ONE ON FOLD

Basic skirt front

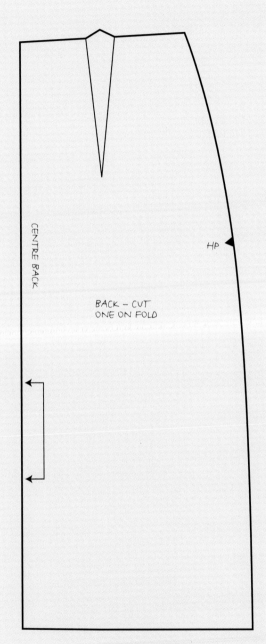

CENTRE BACK

HP

BACK – CUT
ONE ON FOLD

Basic skirt back

making a dress block

It is simplicity itself to create a dress block using your bodice and skirt blocks.

1 Lay out your front bodice and front skirt blocks on the work surface. Line up the centre front lines and have the sides just touching, as shown.

2 Draw a straight vertical line on a new piece of drafting paper then place the paper over the blocks, lining up the drawn line with the centre front lines.

3 Trace the waist darts on the bodice and the skirt, then draw in the missing sections to create a double-ended dart.

4 Draw a smooth line from the side seam of the bodice to the side seam of the skirt.

5 Trace the rest of the bodice and skirt blocks, remembering to include all the relevant pattern markings.

6 Repeat Steps 1–5 using the back bodice and back skirt blocks to make the back dress block.

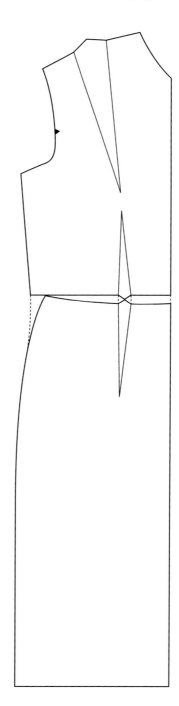
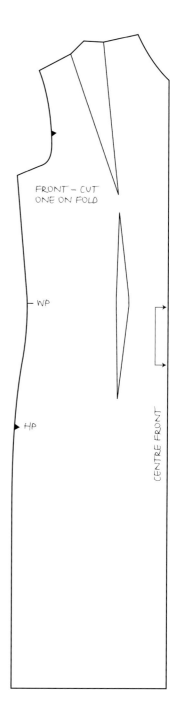

FRONT – CUT ONE ON FOLD

WP

HP

CENTRE FRONT

making a loose sleeve block

The fitted sleeve block can easily be adapted to make a versatile loose sleeve block.

1 Cut a piece of drafting paper larger than the fitted sleeve block. Trace the fitted sleeve, marking in the centre line and the elbow line.

2 Draw a rectangle around the sleeve. The top of the rectangle should touch the shoulder point, the sides of the rectangle touch the underarm side seams and the bottom runs along the wrist line.

3 Draw a line 2.5cm (1 in) up from the wrist line and continue it out 12mm (½ in) beyond the sides of the rectangle.

4 On each side, draw a straight line down from the underarm point to the end of the new wrist line drawn in Step 2; these will become the new underarm seams.

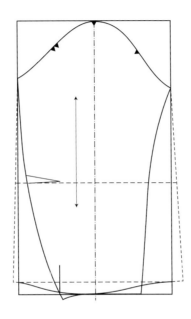

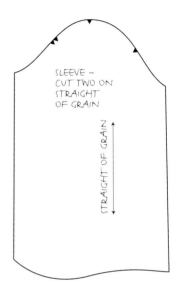

SLEEVE – CUT TWO ON STRAIGHT OF GRAIN

STRAIGHT OF GRAIN

5 Draw in a new wrist line, curving it as shown in the diagram.

6 Add all relevant pattern markings.

sleeve styles

The fitted sleeve is not only useful in its own right, it is also the basis for other sleeves, such as the Ruched Sleeve (see page 86) and the Flared Sleeve (see page 89). Turning the fitted sleeve into a loose sleeve expands the repertoire of sleeve styles you can easily make; for example, the Bell Sleeve (see page 84) and the Bishop Sleeve (see page 88).

making a trouser block

You can draft a trouser block from your skirt block. The steps may look complex, but take your time and follow them carefully and you will find the process easier than you might think.

you will need

- Tape measure
- Flat surface large enough to work on
- Front and back skirt blocks
- Long rule
- Pencil
- Large sheet of drafting paper

Body measurements required

See also page 10.

Outside leg: taken from the natural waistline down to the ankle, usually using the bone on the outside of the ankle as a landmark.

Body rise: sit upright on a flat surface then measure from the natural waistline down to the surface being sat upon.

Trouser bottom width: this is personal choice; 33cm (13 in) tends to produce a classic tailored look.

Front and back block construction lines

1 Lay out the front and back skirt blocks with the side seams close together and parallel. The centre front and back lines should also be parallel and the hip lines on the same horizontal line. Lay the drafting paper over the blocks, ensuring that there is enough paper to draw the entire leg length.

2 Measure the body rise down from the waistline and add 2.5cm (1 in) to this depth. Draw a horizontal line at this depth, marking as point A the place where the line crosses the side seams.

3 Measure the outside leg length down from waistline. Draw a horizontal line across at this depth, marking it line B.

4 Draw a line halfway between point A and line B. This is the knee line, mark it as as line C.

5 On the front and back pieces, draw a vertical line down from waistline to line B. The lines must run centrally through the front and back darts. These are the straight of grain lines.

Back block construction lines

6 On the centre back line raise the waistline by 2.5cm (1 in) and mark this as point D.

7 On line A, the body rise depth, divide the width of the skirt by two. Using this measurement, measure out from the centre back line along line A and mark point E.

8 Divide the measurement from the centre back line to point E by two and mark point F.

9 Draw a dotted line running from point D to point F.

continued overleaf ➤ ➤ ➤

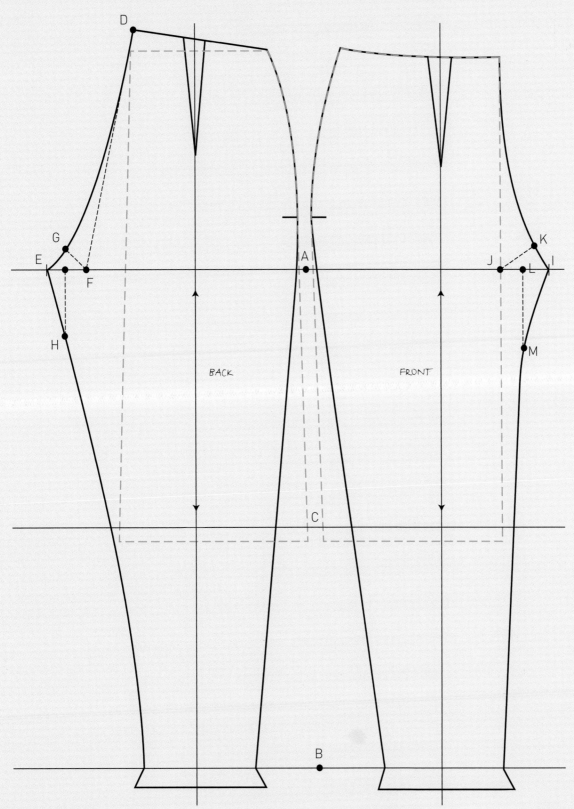

BACK

FRONT

10 From point F draw a line running upwards at 45 degrees to line A. This line must be 3.8cm (1½ in) long and you mark the end of it as point G.

11 Divide the measurement between F and E by two. At this halfway point, draw a vertical line running downwards for 15cm (6 in) and mark the end as point H.

Front block construction lines

12 Take the measurement gained in Step 8 (centre back line to point E, divided by two) and measure out this distance from the centre front along line A. Mark this point I.

13 Mark point J where line A and the centre front line meet.

hipsters

To make hipster trousers, trace the pattern taking 5–10cm (2–4 in) off the waistline. Make a self-faced waistband (see page 122) to fit the top of the new pattern.

14 From point J draw a line running upwards at 45 degrees to line A. This line must be 3.8cm (1½ in) long and you mark the end of it as point K.

15 Divide the measurement between I and J by two. Mark this halfway point as point L. From L, draw a vertical line running downwards for 15cm (6 in) and mark the end of it as point M.

Drawing back trouser block

16 Draw a line from the side seam to point D and extend the dart to meet this new waistline.

17 Follow the curve of the skirt block side seam down to the hip point.

18 On line C, the knee line, measure out 10cm (4 in) from either side of the vertical straight of grain line and mark the ends.

19 On line B, the outside leg length, measure out 7.5cm (3 in) from either side of the vertical straight of grain line and mark the ends.

20 To create the outside seam, draw a straight line from the hip through the point on line C (Step 18) to the point on line B (Step 19).

21 To create the centre back seam, draw a curved line as shown from points D to E, passing through point G.

22 Draw a curved line as shown down from point E to the points on line C marked in Steps 18–19, ensuring the line passes through point H.

23 Draw down from the knee line to the point on line B that was marked in Step 19.

Drawing front trouser block

24 Draw in the dart and the curved waistline from the skirt block.

25 To create the outside seam, follow the curve of the skirt block side seam down to the hip point.

26 On line C, the knee line, measure out 11.5cm (4½ in) from either side of the vertical straight of grain line and mark the ends.

27 On line B, the outside leg length, measure out 9cm (3½ in) from either side of the vertical straight of grain line and mark the ends.

28 To create the outside leg seam, draw a straight line down from the hip through the point on line C that was marked in Step 26 to the point on line B that was marked in Step 27.

29 From the centre front line at the waist draw a curved line as shown down to point I, passing through point K, this will be the new centre front line.

30 Draw a curved line as shown down from point I to the point on line C that was marked in Step 26, ensuring the line passes through point M. Continue the line down to the point on line B that was marked in Step 27; this will be the inside leg seam.

To make facings

To make the facings, fold the paper back on itself along the line B and trace the lower 2.5cm (1 in) of the leg pattern. Fold the paper flat again and trace the facings onto the right side.

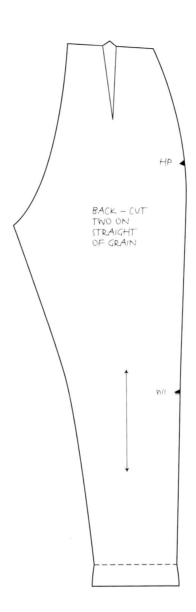

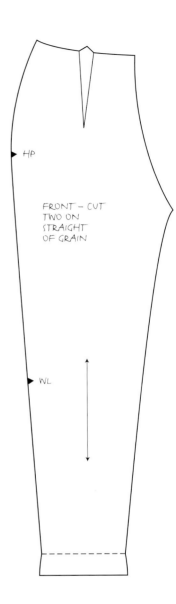

BACK – CUT TWO ON STRAIGHT OF GRAIN

FRONT – CUT TWO ON STRAIGHT OF GRAIN

HP

WL

leg width

The width of the leg at knee and ankle can be increased or decreased as desired: the measurements given here are for guidance only. However, the front of the trouser pattern at knee and ankle should be 2.5cm (1 in) wider than the back to ensure that the trousers hang well.

Creating your Wardrobe

On the following pages you will find a range of garments from a simple, fitted top to sophisticated wide-leg trousers to a strappy summer sundress. To make them you will need your paper blocks (see pages 50–63), drafting paper, long rule, tape measure, pencil, scissors and glue or sticky tape.

The tops

The sleeves

The skirts

The trousers

The dresses

Fitted Top With Button Front
A versatile top that would look
great with any of the sleeves from
the gallery on pages 82–83.

Asymmetrical Top With Buttons
This neat, boxy shape works well
as both a sleeveless top or, with
sleeves, as a jacket.

Cowl-neck top This softly draped
neckline can be made in any
lightweight fabric for both day
and evening wear.

the tops gallery

Your basic bodice and dress blocks (see pages 34–37 and 58–59) can be adapted
to make any of these tops; just follow the instructions to create a pattern.

Top With Ruched Centre Front
Cute made in cotton or glamorous made in silk, this is a versatile top that also looks good with sleeves.

Sun Top With Straps A light, flirty top that can be worn to the beach, to a party, or just out and about enjoying the summer sun.

Wrap-over Top A style that flatters most figures, wrap-overs can be made to tie at the side or, as here, with the wrap sewn into the seam.

Make any of these tops in cool cotton for summer wear, add sleeves and use warm wool for winter, or choose a special fabric for an evening outfit.

fitted top with button front

Based on the Basic Dress Block (see pages 58–59), this versatile top can be worn sleeveless or, as demonstrated in the Sleeve Gallery (see pages 82–83), with any of the sleeve designs, each of which give it a completely different look.

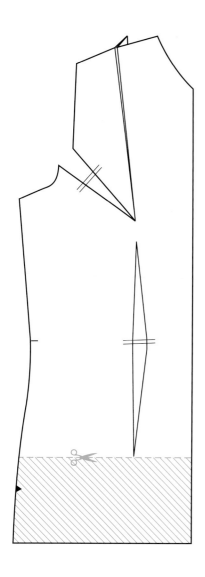

1 Overlay the basic dress front block with drafting paper and trace it to just below the hip point. Set the dress block aside.

2 Cut across the traced pattern at the desired hem; on this sample it is just above the hip line.

3 Throw the shoulder-to-bust dart (see page 55) to create a dart that comes from the armhole.

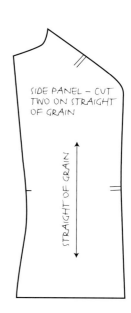

SIDE PANEL – CUT TWO ON STRAIGHT OF GRAIN

STRAIGHT OF GRAIN

4 To create the side front section, overlay the pattern with a new piece of drafting paper and trace along the lower edge of the armhole dart to the point of the waist-to-bust dart, then along the left-hand side of this dart to the hem. Then trace along the hem to the side seam, up the side seam and around the lower armhole section.

5 Add 1.5cm (⅝ in) seam allowances, a hem and relevant pattern markings.

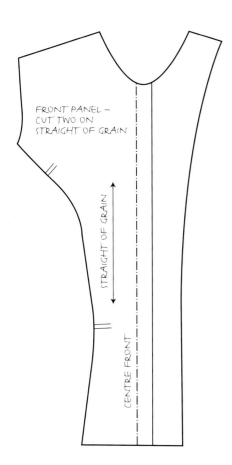

FRONT PANEL –
CUT TWO ON
STRAIGHT OF GRAIN

STRAIGHT OF GRAIN

CENTRE FRONT

6 To create the centre front section, overlay the pattern with a new piece of drafting paper and trace along other side of both darts, along the hem, up the centre front line, around the neck and shoulder line and around the armhole.

Add a button stand (making sure it is wide enough for your buttons).

7 Fold the paper back on itself along the straight edge of the button stand and create a facing, as shown.

8 Add 1.5cm (⅝ in) seam allowances, a hem and relevant pattern markings.

9 As a front facing has been created, a back neck facing will also be required (see page 119).

10 Trace the basic dress back to the same length as the front to make the back of this top.

11 Add 1.5cm (⅝ in) seam allowances, a hem and relevant pattern markings.

12 To neaten the armholes either create a facing (see page 118), or finish them with bias binding (see pages 28-29).

button stand

The button stand is simply an extension of the bodice front beyond the centre front line and is added to both the left- and right-hand sides. On one side it will have the buttonholes and will overlap; on the other side it will have the buttons and will underlap. It's usually best to interface the buttonstand to give it some structure (see page 16).

asymmetrical top with buttons

This looks great as a short summer top or you can make it in a heavier fabric and add sleeves to turn it into a little jacket.

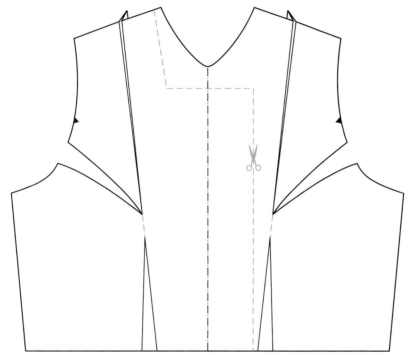

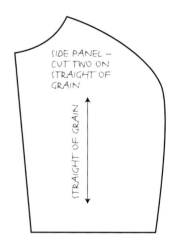

SIDE PANEL –
CUT TWO ON
STRAIGHT OF
GRAIN

STRAIGHT OF GRAIN

1 Overlay the basic bodice block (see pages 34–41) with drafting paper and trace it. Then flip the block and trace it again to create a complete front block.

2 Draw in a curved line from the armhole to the top of the waist dart, ensuring you pass through the end of the bust dart coming from the shoulder.

3 Cut along this line until you reach the tip of the shoulder-to-bust dart. Fold out the shoulder-to-bust dart.

4 Draw in the new neckline and the overlap, as shown.

5 To create the side front section, overlay the pattern with a new piece of drafting paper and trace the side section. Draw along the lower edge of the new dart, down the left-hand side of the waist dart, along the waist, up the side seam and around the bottom section of the arm.

6 Add 1.5cm (⅝ in) seam allowances, a hem and relevant pattern markings.

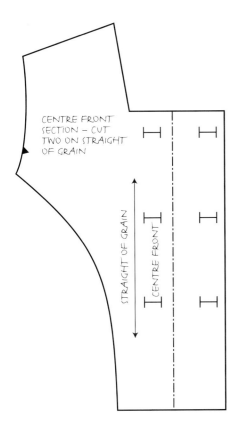

CENTRE FRONT SECTION – CUT TWO ON STRAIGHT OF GRAIN

STRAIGHT OF GRAIN

CENTRE FRONT

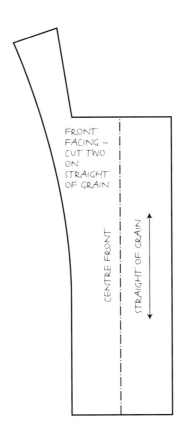

FRONT FACING – CUT TWO ON STRAIGHT OF GRAIN

CENTRE FRONT

STRAIGHT OF GRAIN

7 To create the centre front section, overlay the pattern with a new piece of drafting paper. Trace along the right-hand side of the dart, along the hem, up the centre front and around the upper section of armhole.

8 Add 1.5cm (⅝ in) seam allowances, a hem, the positions of the buttons and relevant pattern markings.

9 To create a facing, overlay the centre front section with a new piece of drafting paper. Trace 7.5cm (3 in) along the hem to the front edge, up the front, around the neckline and along the shoulder line for 7.5cm (3 in), then gently curve down to the hemline.

10 Add 1.5cm (⅝ in) seam allowances, a hem and relevant pattern markings.

11 Trace the basic back bodice without alteration and create a back neck facing (see page 119) to complement the front facing.

12 To neaten the armholes either create a facing (see page 118), or finish them with bias binding (see pages 28-29).

Cowl- neck top

Make this in slinky fabric as a great party top for evenings out when you want to be noticed.

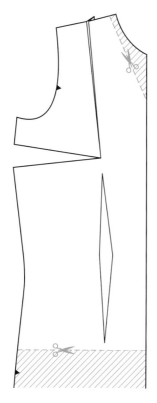

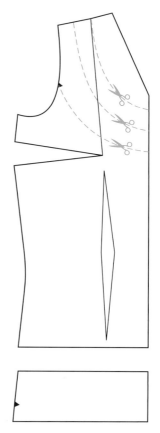

1 Overlay the basic dress block (see page 58) with drafting paper and trace it to the hip point or just above, depending on where you wish the top to finish.

2 Throw the dart into the side seam (see page 55).

3 Cut the neck into a 'V' as deep as you wish the neckline to be.

4 Draw three design lines from the centre front to the shoulder and armhole seams, as shown.

5 Cut along these lines from the centre front to within 2mm (⅛ in) of the far edge

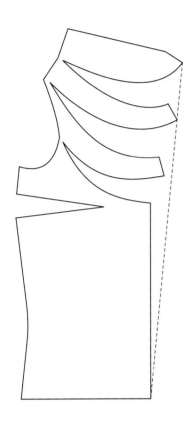

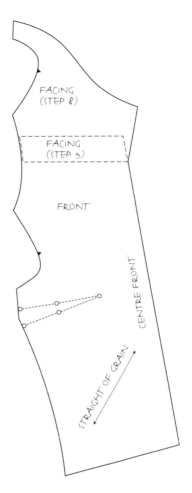

6 Fan out the cut lines; on this sample they are 5cm (2 in) apart.

7 Overlay the pattern with a new piece of drafting paper and trace around the hem, up the side seam, around the arm hole and along the top of the neck. Draw a straight line from the edge of the neck down to the hem to create a new centre front line.

8 To create the facing (if it is a sleeveless top), fold the paper back on itself and trace along the shoulder seam, around the armhole, down the side seam for 5cm (2 in), across to the centre front line and up to the neckline. With this facing you will need to cut two fronts and seam them.

9 To create the facing (if it is a sleeved top) fold the paper back on itself and trace a band 10cm (4 in) wide, as shown by the dotted lines on the diagram. With this facing you can cut one front on the fold.

10 Add 1.5cm (⅝ in) seam allowances, a hem and relevant pattern markings. The drape of this top is improved if it is cut on the true bias of the fabric, so here the straight of grain line is shown running at 45 degrees to the centre front line.

11 Trace the basic dress back to the same length as the front in Step 1 to make the back of this top. You can make a cowl neckline as for the front if you wish.

12 Add 1.5cm (⅝ in) seam allowances, a hem and relevant pattern markings.

top with ruched centre front

This lovely top flatters a range of figures and looks good made in cotton for day wear or something special for the evening.

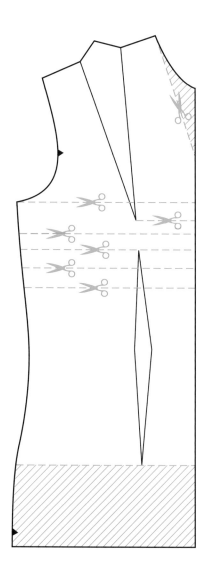

1 Overlay the basic dress block (see page 58) with drafting paper and trace it to where you wish the top to finish.

2 Cut the neck into a 'V' as deep as you wish the neckline to be.

3 From the centre front line draw two horizontal design lines, the first running across the shoulder-to-bust dart to the bottom of the armhole and the second to the point of this dart.

4 For extra ruching, draw additional lines from the centre front line across to the side seam, as shown.

gathering

Use the technique for gathering the head of a fitted sleeve (see page 23) to gather up the two front edges of this top. Using short tacking stitches, gather as marked on the pattern. Then tack the fronts together, matching the gathered sections. Finally machine-sew the front seam.

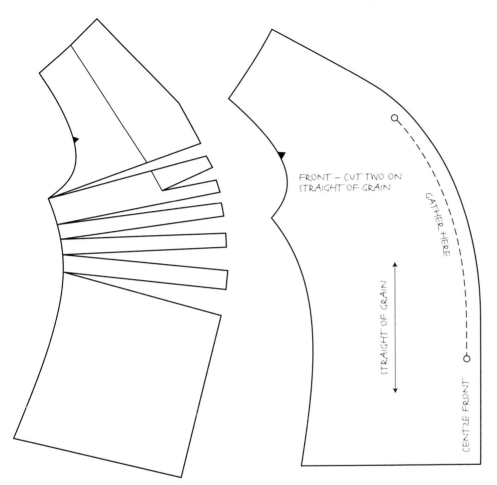

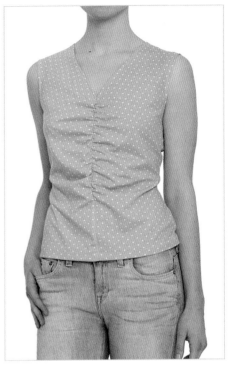

FRONT – CUT TWO ON
STRAIGHT OF GRAIN

STRAIGHT OF GRAIN

GATHER HERE

CENTRE FRONT

5 Cut along the first two lines and fold out the dart.

6 Cut and open out the remaining lines. The wider the cuts are opened, the more ruched the front will be.

7 Overlay the pattern with a new piece of drafting paper and trace the pattern. Add 1.5cm (⅝ in) seam allowances, a hem and relevant pattern markings.

8 Trace the basic dress back to the same length as the front to make the back of this top.

9 Add 1.5cm (⅝ in) seam allowances, a hem and relevant pattern markings.

10 To neaten the armholes either create a facing (see page 118), or finish them with bias binding (see page 28).

Sun top with Straps

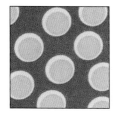

This summer top can be dressed up with a gorgeous skirt or dressed down with a pair of jeans.

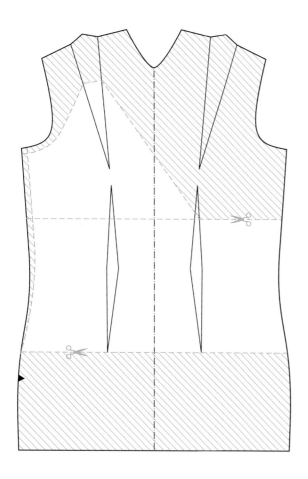

To create the front pattern

1 Overlay the basic dress block (see page 58) with drafting paper and trace it. Then flip the block and trace it again to create a complete front block.

2 Draw a line across the pattern where you wish the hemline to be.

3 Measure in 1.5cm (⅝ in) under the arm and 5mm (¼ in) at the waist and move the side seam in to these marks.

4 Draw a line across the bodice where you want the under-bust line to be.

5 Drop the underarm point by 1cm (½ in). Decide how high you wish the highest point on the top to be (this will be the position of the strap) and mark this on the shoulder bust dart.

6 Draw a gentle curve from the new underarm point to the marked top point on the left-hand side of the shoulder dart, then draw straight across the dart. Continue the line down to the middle of the opposite waist dart, meeting the under-bust line drawn in Step 4. Cut along these design lines to cut out the bra section and the skirt section.

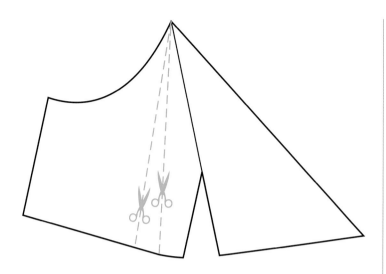

7 On the new bra section, cut up the lower bust dart and fold out the dart. Then cut two extra vertical lines from the bust line to the shoulder point. Fan these out to give extra gather.

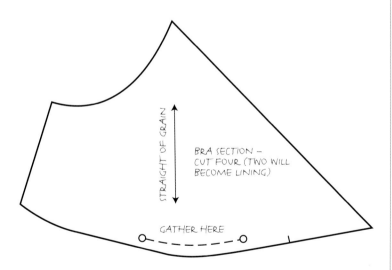

STRAIGHT OF GRAIN

BRA SECTION –
CUT FOUR (TWO WILL
BECOME LINING)

GATHER HERE

8 Overlay the pattern with a new piece of drafting paper and trace the new pattern. Add 1.5cm (⅝ in) seam allowances and relevant pattern markings.

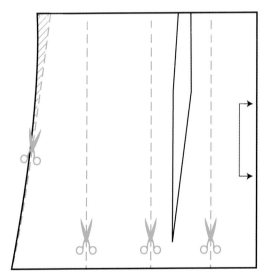

9 On the skirt section of the top, trim the side seam by the width of the dart.

continued next page ➤ ➤ ➤

the tops 77

10 Draw three evenly spaced lines running vertically up from the hem. Cut along these lines to within 2mm (⅛ in) of the bust line and fan them out. The wider the fan, the more flared the skirt section will be.

To create the back pattern

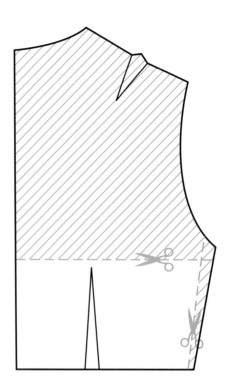

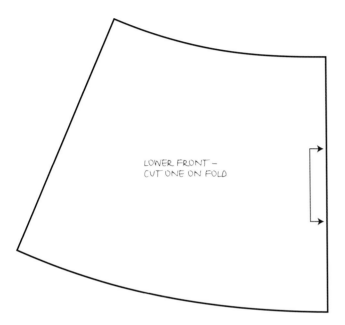

LOWER FRONT –
CUT ONE ON FOLD

11 Overlay the pattern with a new piece of drafting paper and trace the new pattern. Add 1.5cm (⅝ in) seam allowances, a hem and relevant pattern markings.

12 Trace the basic dress back block. Measure in 1cm (½ in) at the underarm point and 5mm (¼ in) at the waist and draw in a new side seam.

13 Drop the underarm point by 1cm (½ in) then, using the bust line on the front as the top edge, work out the design lines for the back top section. Fold out the dart.

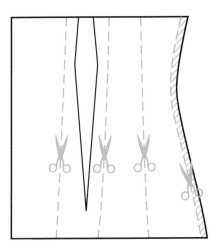

14 Adjust the side seam and fan out the back skirt section as for the front skirt section.

16 Measure how long you need the straps to be.

17 Draw a rectangle that is the measured length and double the width you wish the finished strap to be.

18 Add 1.5cm (⅝ in) seam allowances and label the section 'straps - cut two on straight of grain'.

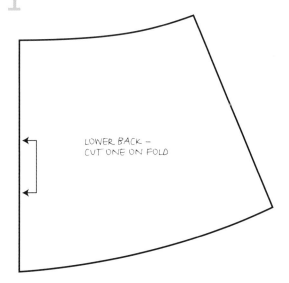

LOWER BACK – CUT ONE ON FOLD

zips and hems

This pattern would need a side zip running from under the arm down into the middle of the skirt section. If you prefer a centre back zip, the back section will have to be cut out in two parts.

As this top has a flared hem it is advisable to have a smaller hem than usual, perhaps 1.5cm (⅝ in).

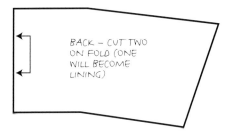

BACK – CUT TWO ON FOLD (ONE WILL BECOME LINING)

15 Overlay the patterns with new pieces of drafting paper and trace them. Add 1.5cm (⅝ in) seam allowances, a hem and relevant pattern markings.

Wrap-Over top

This top is very forgiving for rounder tummies if you make it so that it ties up at the side; you can then adjust the ties to skim the tummy.

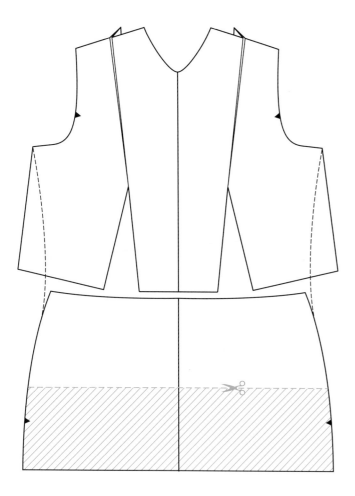

◀ 1 Overlay the basic bodice block (see pages 34–41) with drafting paper and trace it. Then flip the block and trace it again to create a complete front block. Throw the shoulder darts into the waist darts (see page 55).

2 Place the skirt block below this pattern. Lengthen the top to just above the hip point. Draw in new side seams running from the underarm to the top of the skirt, as shown.

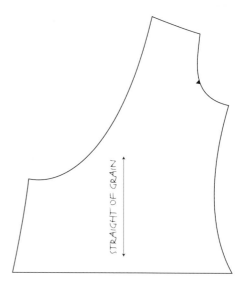

STRAIGHT OF GRAIN

▲ 3 Working on the left-hand side of wear, draw in a new neckline as deep as you wish it to be. Overlay the pattern with a new piece of drafting paper and trace it. Add 1.5cm (⅝ in) seam allowances, a hem and relevant pattern markings.

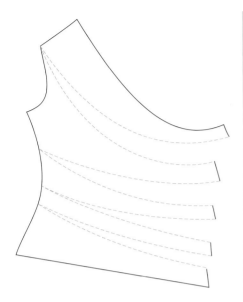

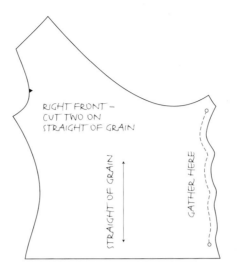

RIGHT FRONT –
CUT TWO ON
STRAIGHT OF GRAIN

STRAIGHT OF GRAIN

GATHER HERE

4 Working on the right-hand side of wear, draw in a new neckline as deep as you wish it to be. Then draw four curved lines from the side seam up to the opposite shoulder and side seam.

5 Cut along these lines and fan out the sections to create the extra fabric that will be gathered up into the side seam.

6 Overlay the pattern with a new piece of drafting paper and trace it. Add 1.5cm (⅝ in) seam allowances, a hem and relevant pattern markings.

7 Overlay the basic bodice back with drafting paper and trace it, making it the same length as the front.

8 To neaten the armholes either create a facing (see page 118), or finish them with bias binding (see page 28-29).

tied at the side

This sample has the wrap-over sewn into the side seam, but you can sew it into a tie section to create a tie front wrap-over, as for the wrap-over dress (see page 100).

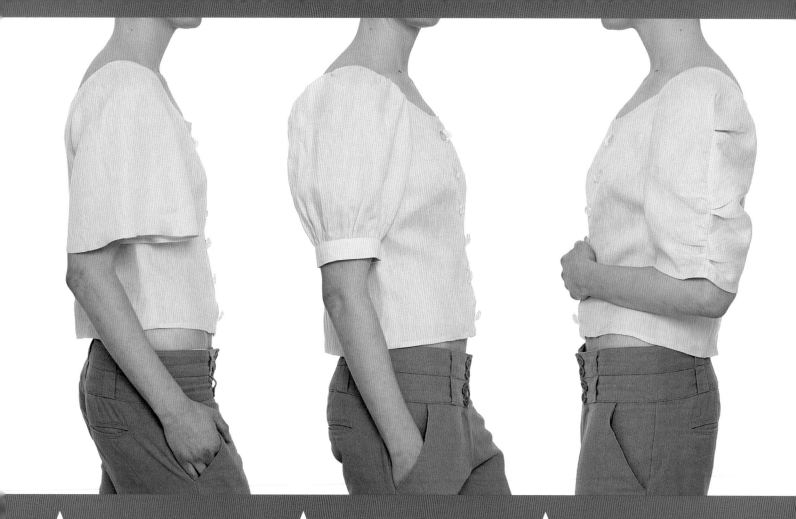

Bell Sleeve An ideal sleeve for summer, this is comfortable and is a great option if you prefer to have your arms covered.

Puff Sleeve Easy to make and wear, this sleeve style also fits in well with the vintage fashions that are so popular.

Ruched Sleeve Made in crisp cotton this sleeve looks fresh and pretty. Made in a soft fabric, it will drape beautifully.

the sleeve gallery

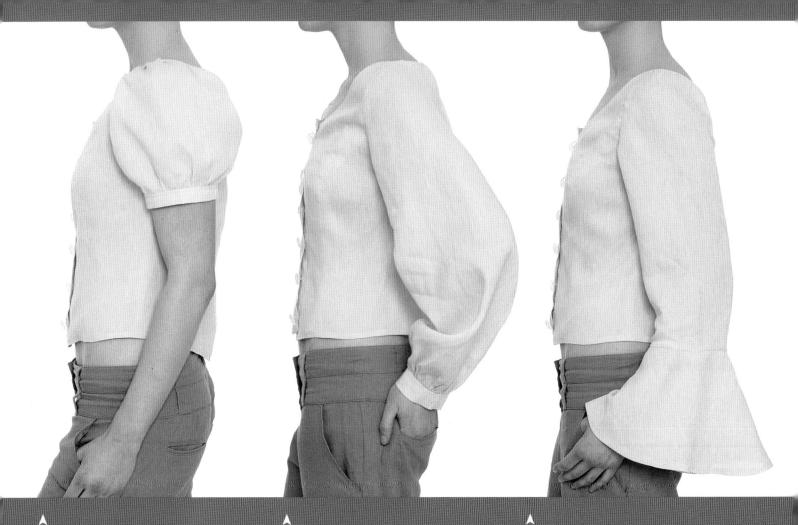

Cap Puff Sleeve Add this sleeve to summer dresses and tops for a casual style that is also very pretty and feminine.

Bishop Sleeve Comfortable and yet quite formal, this is a great sleeve style for office clothes for both summer and winter.

Flared Sleeve A lovely sleeve style that is ideal for evening wear. Add it to dresses or jackets for a really glamorous look.

Try different sleeves with your basic bodice to see which ones suit your shape best. Adjust length and width and you'll come up with your ideal sleeve style.

bell sleeve

This casual sleeve is ideal if you have larger arms as it is both flattering and comfortable to wear.

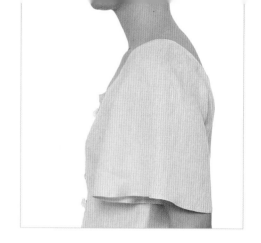

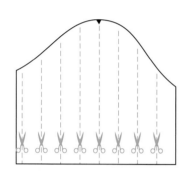

1 Overlay the basic loose sleeve block (see page 59) with drafting paper and trace it to the desired length: in this sample it is just above the elbow.

2 Draw evenly spaced vertical lines from the hem to the sleeve head. Cut along the lines from the hem upward, stopping 2mm (⅛ in) short of the sleeve head edge.

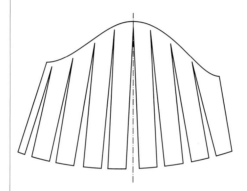

3 On a new piece of drafting paper draw a vertical line; this will be the new centre line. Place the central two sections of the sleeve on either side of this line and fan them out at the hem, spacing them evenly on either side of the centre line. Stick the sections in place. Fan out and stick the other sections in place; as shown: in this sample each gap is 2.5cm (1 in). Widening the gaps will make the sleeve fuller and vice versa.

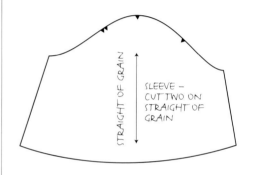

4 Overlay the pattern with a new piece of drafting paper and trace it. Add 1.5cm (⅝ in) seam allowances, a hem and relevant pattern markings.

STRAIGHT OF GRAIN

SLEEVE – CUT TWO ON STRAIGHT OF GRAIN

puff sleeve

To make this full sleeve, gathered at shoulder and cuff, all you need to do is add extra width to your basic sleeve block shape.

1 Overlay the basic fitted sleeve block (see page 42) with drafting paper and trace it to the desired length. Cut across, allowing for the cuff.

2 Working either side of the centre line, draw vertical lines from the head to the base of the sleeve. Here, the lines are 4cm (1½ in) apart, but you can place them further apart or closer together.

3 Cut the sleeve along these lines and number each section.

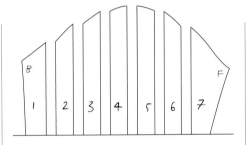

4 On a new piece of paper, draw a horizontal line long enough to accommodate all the pieces.

5 Glue each piece in place, ensuring the bottom edge is placed on the line. Place them as far apart as you like. Here the gap between each section is 2cm (¾ in).

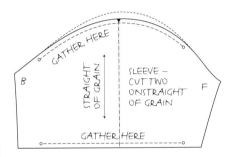

6 Overlay the pattern with a new piece of drafting paper and trace it. Add 1.5cm (⅝ in) seam allowances and relevant pattern markings. If you wish, you can add a little extra fullness at the top of the sleeve, as shown by the dotted line.

to draft the cuff

SLEEVE BAND – CUT 2

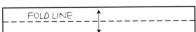

1 To work out how long your cuff should be, measure around your bicep while your arm is bent, then add 1cm (½ in) for comfort.

2 Draft the cuff twice the width you want and add 1.5cm (⅝ in) seam allowance on all sides. (See also page 123.)

ruched sleeve

This sleeve will look great with any of the bodices in this book, but works especially well with the ruched top on page 74.

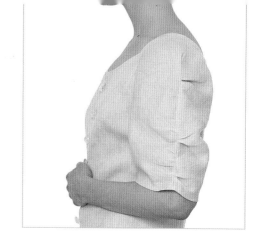

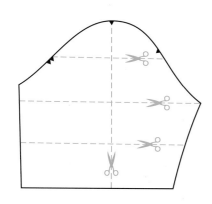

1 Overlay the basic fitted sleeve block (see page 42) with drafting paper and trace it to the desired length: in this sample it is just above the elbow.

2 Draw in the centre line running down the sleeve from the apex of the sleeve head. Then draw three evenly spaced horizontal lines across the sleeve.

3 Cut up the centre line to within 2mm (⅛ in) of the sleeve head. From the centre cut, cut along the horizontal lines to within 2mm (⅛ in) of the edges.

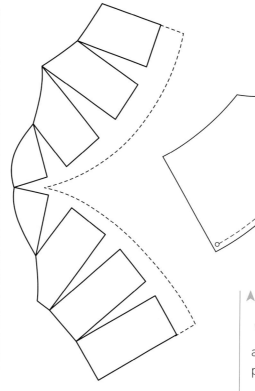

4 Fan the sleeve out to create the desired gather. On this sample the ends of the central cut are 2.5cm (1 in) apart and the ends of the horizontal cuts are 4cm (1½ in) apart. For a fuller sleeve, add 4cm (1½ in) to the inner width of the sleeve at the hem and taper this towards the sleeve head, as shown by the dotted line.

5 Overlay the pattern with a new piece of drafting paper and trace it. Add 1.5cm (⅝ in) seam allowances, a hem and relevant pattern markings.

6 If you want to reduce the amount of fabric needed to make the sleeve, cut the pattern in half right up to the sleeve head, as shown by the dotted line. Add a seam allowance and cut out the sleeve in two separate pieces.

Cap puff sleeve

This is a lovely sleeve for summer dresses and tops. It can be made a little longer if you prefer.

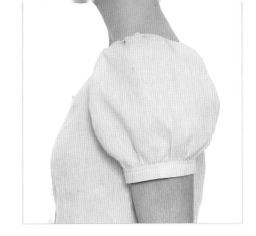

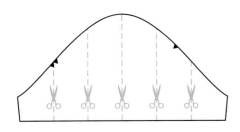

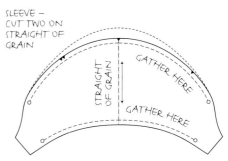

SLEEVE –
CUT TWO ON
STRAIGHT OF
GRAIN

STRAIGHT OF GRAIN

GATHER HERE

GATHER HERE

1 Overlay the basic fitted sleeve block (see page 42) with drafting paper and trace it to the desired length; in this sample it is 5cm (2 in) from the underarm point.

2 Draw five evenly spaced lines running vertically from the arm opening to the sleeve head. Number each section then cut along the lines to separate the sections.

3 On a new piece of drafting paper draw a vertical line; this will be the new centre line. Evenly space the cut sections on either side of the centre line, as shown. The wider spacing at the sleeve head gives it more flare than the arm opening.

4 Overlay the pattern with a new piece of drafting paper and trace it. If you want to increase the fullness of the sleeve head, add an extra 2.5cm (1 in) in height at the centre of the sleeve head, tapering it down to nothing at the sides, as shown by the dotted line. Add 1.5cm (⅝ in) seam allowances and relevant pattern markings.

5 Create a band cuff following the instructions on page 85. To work out how long the band needs to be, bend your arm and measure around the bicep, then add 1cm (½ in) for comfort.

choosing fabric

This style of sleeve is best made in a fairly lightweight fabric that has a natural crispness. If you use a heavyweight fabric or a soft fabric then you may not get a perfectly puffed sleeve. For day wear you could use a cotton fabric and for evening wear, try dupioni silk.

bishop sleeve

This is a simple-to-make sleeve that is ideal on a dress or top when you need to look smart.

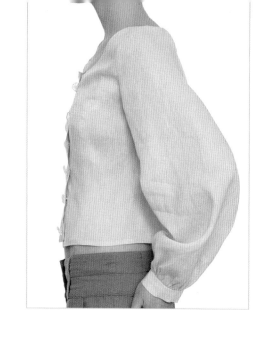

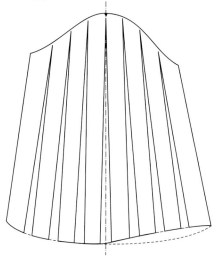

1 Overlay the basic loose sleeve block (see page 59) with drafting paper and trace it. Draw evenly spaced vertical lines from wrist to shoulder: in this sample the lines are 4cm (1½ in) apart.

2 Cut up the lines to within 2mm (⅛ in) of the sleeve head. On a second piece of drafting paper draw a vertical line slightly longer than the sleeve.

3 Match the shoulder point with the top of the line then begin to space out the wrist line evenly, sticking the sections in place as you work. In this sample the sections are spaced 2.5cm (1 in) apart.

4 If extra fullness is required at the base then drop the front section of the sleeve by 2.5cm (1 in), tapering to nothing at the centre line and the front seam, as shown by the dotted line.

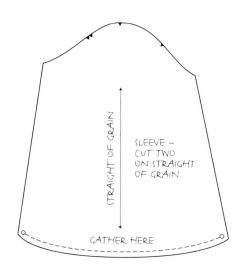

STRAIGHT OF GRAIN

SLEEVE –
CUT TWO
ON STRAIGHT
OF GRAIN

GATHER HERE

5 Overlay the pattern with a new piece of drafting paper and trace it. Add 1.5cm (⅝ in) seam allowances and relevant pattern markings.

FOLD LINE

6 Follow the instructions for creating a cuff band on page 85, ensuring that the cuff will easily fit over the hand.

flared sleeve

You'll be surprised how simple this elegant sleeve is to make. Draft a flared cuff that is then sewn to the basic fitted sleeve shape.

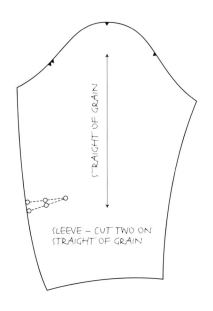

SLEEVE – CUT TWO ON STRAIGHT OF GRAIN

STRAIGHT OF GRAIN

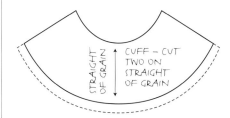

STRAIGHT OF GRAIN

CUFF – CUT TWO ON STRAIGHT OF GRAIN

1 Overlay the basic fitted sleeve block (see page 42) with drafting paper and trace it. Draw a horizontal line where you wish the cuff to start: on this sample it is 15cm (6 in) up from the wrist. Cut off the lower section of the sleeve and set the upper section aside.

2 On the lower section of the sleeve draw five equally spaced lines from the wrist to the top of the cuff section.

3 Cut up these lines to within 2mm (⅛ in) of the top.

4 Fan out the bottom section of the cuff to desired amount; this sample has a flare of 4cm (1½ in) between each cut section

5 Overlay the cut cuff with a piece of drafting paper and trace the new pattern. You can add a little extra length so that the cuffs hangs down over the hand, as shown by the dotted line

6 Add pattern markings, 1.5cm (⅝ in) seam allowances and a hem (see page 53) to both sections.

The Flared Skirt Simplicity itself, this skirt is quick to make and will work well in both summer cottons and winter wools.

The Wrap-over Skirt An easy-to-wear style that looks good on all shapes and sizes and in almost any type of fabric.

Skirt With Godets Fitted around the hips, this skirt has inset pieces that allow it to flare out gently towards the hem.

the skirt and trouser gallery

Your versatile draped calico skirt block can be adapted to make a trouser pattern (see pages 60–63) then it's simple to make all of these garments.

Boot-cut Trousers These versatile trousers look great on all types of figures because they elongate the leg and flatter the waist.

Wide-legTrousers Looking good in pinstripes for the office or velvet for the evening, these trousers will be in your wardrobe all year round.

Capri Pants Chic and comfortable to wear, these are the perfect trousers for summer, whether you are on the beach or at a party.

Whether you need a cotton wrap-over skirt for your summer vacation or stylish trousers to wear to work, there's an easy-to-make pattern here.

flared skirt

This is a timeless skirt that looks good at any length and can be made from the lightest of cottons to the heaviest of wools.

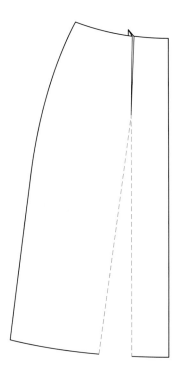

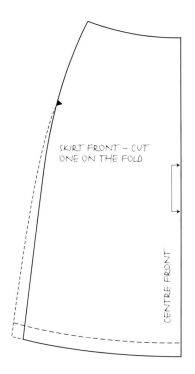

SKIRT FRONT – CUT
ONE ON THE FOLD

CENTRE FRONT

1 Overlay the basic skirt front (see pages 46–49) block with drafting paper and trace it. Draw a vertical line running from the point of the dart to the hem. Cut up this line from the hem to the point of the dart.

2 Fold out the waist dart so that the pattern opens up along the cut line to give the flare needed.

3 Overlay the pattern with a new piece of drafting paper and trace it, smoothing out the hip line. If more flare is required add a further 2.5cm (1 in) on the side seam, starting from the hip line, as shown by the dotted line.

4 To create the contrast band around the hem, draw a line across the hem at the required depth, as shown by the dashed line. Cut off this section to make a separate pattern piece.

5 Add 1.5cm (⅝ in) seam allowances, a 5cm (2 in) hem and relevant pattern markings.

6 Repeat Steps 1–5 with the back skirt block to make a back skirt.

7 Create a waistband (see page 122). The zip will be in the left-hand side seam.

boot-cut trousers

An ever-fashionable and flattering trouser style that looks great with shoes or boots.

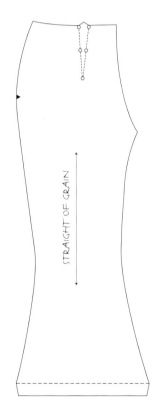

STRAIGHT OF GRAIN

1 Overlay the basic trouser block (see pages 60–63) with drafting paper and trace it to knee level.

2 Draw in the hem line. Decide how wide you want the flare, then extend the hem to the desired width.

3 Draw in a curved line, as shown by the dotted line, from the knee the new hem.

4 Fold the paper back on itself at the hem and trace a 5cm (2 in) facing.

5 Overlay the pattern with a new piece of drafting paper and trace it. Add 1.5cm (⅝ in) seam allowances and relevant pattern markings.

6 Repeat the process for the back, ensuring that the flare starts at the same position as for the front. Make sure that all matching seams are the same length to avoid problems when making up the trousers.

7 Create a waistband (see page 122). The zip will be in the left-hand side seam.

Wrap-over Skirt

This skirt is ideal for all ages and for all seasons. It can be made from light cotton for summer or wool for winter.

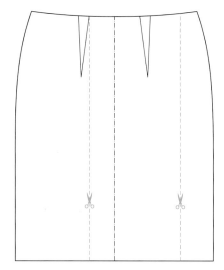

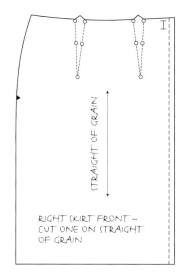

RIGHT SKIRT FRONT – CUT ONE ON STRAIGHT OF GRAIN

STRAIGHT OF GRAIN

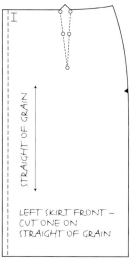

STRAIGHT OF GRAIN

LEFT SKIRT FRONT – CUT ONE ON STRAIGHT OF GRAIN

1 Overlay the basic skirt front block (see pages 46–49) with drafting paper and trace it. Flip the block and trace it again to create a complete skirt front block.

2 Decide how far you want the over section to wrap over; in this sample it covers two-thirds of the left-hand side. Draw a vertical line from waist to hem at this point.

3 Decide how far you want the under section to wrap under; here, it lies under one-third of the right-hand side. Draw a line from the waist to the hem at this point.

4 Overlay the pattern with a new piece of drafting paper and trace the right-hand side of the skirt from the side seam to the line drawn in Step 2. This will be the over wrap section.

5 Add a 2.5cm (1 in) facing along the front edge, 1.5cm (⅝ in) seam allowances, a 5cm (2 in) hem and relevant pattern markings. This sample uses a button to fasten the skirt, but you could use ties.

6 Repeat Steps 4 and 5 for the left-hand side, tracing the pattern from the side seam to the line drawn in Step 3. This will be the under wrap section.

7 Copy the basic skirt back block without alteration. Add 1.5cm (⅝ in) seam allowances, a 5cm (2 in) hem and pattern markings.

8 Create a self-facing waistband (see page 122).

wide-leg trousers

These trousers are great for a range of occasions and they are so versatile because you can dress them up or down as needed.

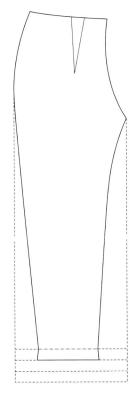

STRAIGHT OF GRAIN

TROUSER FRONT –
CUT TWO ON
STRAIGHT OF GRAIN

1 Overlay the basic trouser block (see pages 60–63) with drafting paper and trace it to the hip point and top of the inside leg seam.

2 From the hip point, draw a vertical line down to the original hem line.

3 From the top of the inside leg seam, draw a vertical line down to the original hem line.

4 Draw in the hem line and extend it out to the new side and inside leg seams.

5 Extend the side and inside leg seams to run 7.5cm (3 in) below the hem line.

6 Draw a horizontal line 2.5cm (1 in) below the hem. This will be the first section of the turn-up.

7 Draw another line 2.5cm (1 in) below the first. This will be the second part of the turn-up. The final 2.5cm (1 in) will be the hem.

8 Overlay the pattern with a new piece of drafting paper and trace it. Add 1.5cm (⅝ in) seam allowances and pattern markings.

9 Repeat the process for the back, ensuring the flare starts at the same position as for the front.

10 Create a waistband (see page 122). The zip will be in the left-hand side seam.

skirt with godets

This is an elegant skirt that has a lovely movement as you walk. It looks great knee length (as in this sample), but equally great at calf length or to the ankle.

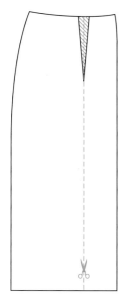

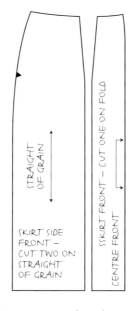

STRAIGHT OF GRAIN

SKIRT SIDE FRONT – CUT TWO ON STRAIGHT OF GRAIN

SKIRT FRONT – CUT ONE ON FOLD

CENTRE FRONT

1 Overlay the basic skirt front block (see pages 46–49) with drafting paper and trace it. Draw a vertical line through the middle of the waist dart and down to the hem.

2 Cut up this line to the point of the dart then cut up both sides of the dart. This removes the dart and a seam will replace it.

3 Add 1.5cm (⅝ in) seam allowances, a 5cm (2 in) hem and relevant pattern markings to both pieces.

4 Repeat Steps 1–3 with the basic skirt back block, labeling the pieces appropriately.

5 Create a waistband (see page 122). The zip will be in the left-hand side seam.

6 On drafting paper, draw a vertical line the length of the godet. Mark the top '1' and the bottom '2'. Draw a horizontal line at '2'.

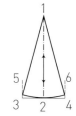

7 Halve the desired width of the godet. Take this measurement out to each side from '2' and mark '3' and '4'. Draw vertical lines running up from '3' and '4'.

8 Position a rule so the zero is on '1' and check the length from '1' to '2'. Keeping the zero in place, pivot the rule until the same measurement touches the vertical line coming from '3' and mark this '5'. Repeat on the other side, marking '6'.

9 Draw in the bottom curve of the godet, starting at '5', curving to '2', then to '6'. Add 1.5cm (⅝ in) seam allowances, a 5cm (2 in) hem and label it 'godet – cut 6 on straight of grain'.

capri pants

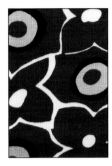

These trousers are simple to sew and are great for packing away for your summer holiday in the sun.

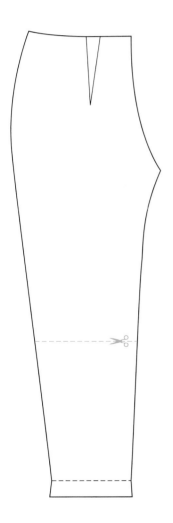

1 Overlay the basic trouser block (see pages 60–63) with drafting paper and trace it down to where you want the hem to be; in this sample it is mid-calf.

2 Draw a horizontal line at this point for the new hem line.

3 Fold the paper back on itself along the hem line and trace a 5cm (2 in) facing. Fold the paper flat and trace the lines onto the right side.

4 Add 1.5cm (⅝ in) seam allowances and relevant pattern markings.

5 Repeat the process for the back, ensuring that the inside leg and side seams are the same length as the front.

6 Create a waistband (see page 122). The zip will be in the left-hand side seam.

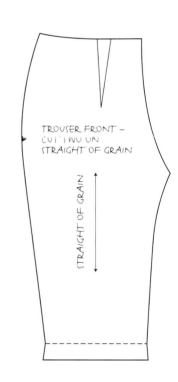

TROUSER FRONT – CUT TWO ON STRAIGHT OF GRAIN

STRAIGHT OF GRAIN

the dress gallery

A great dress pattern that flatters your figure is an asset to any wardrobe because you can do so much with it. In linen or cotton it's a summer outfit, add sleeves and make it in a heavier fabric for winter, or sew it in a special fabric and create a party dress.

Try on different dresses in a shop and see what shape suits you, then adapt your basic dress block to make the perfect fit and style for you.

Wrap-over Dress This is a very flattering style to choose if you have a rounder tummy than you'd like as it skims neatly over the stomach.

Princess-line Dress Show off curves you are proud of with this classic, fitted dress that will look great for work or play.

Sundress With Straps A really lovely, relaxed style that's ideal for summer holidays, either as a day dress or for evenings out

Flared Dress This is a great smart-casual look for summer or, with sleeves added, for winter. Try it with the Bishop Sleeve (see page 88).

Wrap-over dress

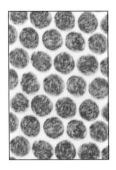

This dress flatters a range of figure types and can be made to look very different by adding sleeves. For example, the Bell Sleeve (see page 84) would work well.

▲1 To make the dress bodice front, overlay the basic bodice block (see pages 34–41) with drafting paper and trace it. Then flip the block and trace it again to create a complete front block. Throw the shoulder-to-bust darts into the side seams (see page 55).

▲2 Starting a short distance down the shoulder line, draw in the design line curve. End the curve on the waist, just short of the side seam (the amount depends on your own preference).

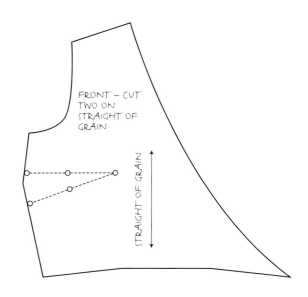

FRONT - CUT
TWO ON
STRAIGHT OF
GRAIN

STRAIGHT OF GRAIN

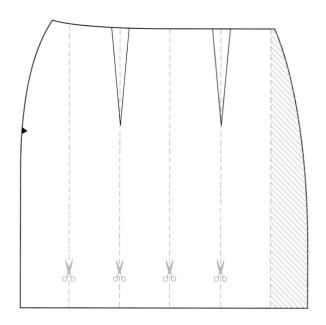

▲3 Add 1.5cm (⅝ in) seam allowances and relevant pattern markings. This pattern piece is for both the left and right fronts.

4 To make the dress bodice back, overlay the basic bodice back block with drafting paper and trace it. Remember to drop the shoulder line by the same amount as for the front.

5 To neaten the armholes and front edges of the bodice, either create facings (see page 118), or finish them with bias binding (see page 28). If you make a facing for the front, then it is best to make one for the back neck.

▲6 To make the ties, draw a rectangle as long as you need the ties to be and twice the width. Add 1.5cm (⅝ in) seam allowances and relevant pattern markings.

▲7 To make the front skirt of the dress, overlay the basic skirt front block (see pages 46–49) with drafting paper and trace it. Then flip the block and trace it again to create a complete front block.

8 Draw in the design line for the skirt, starting at the waist in the same position as the cross over on the top. Cut this section off the pattern.

9 Draw four equally spaced vertical lines running from the hem to the waist. Two of these lines must go through the centres of the waist darts.

continued next page ➤ ➤ ➤

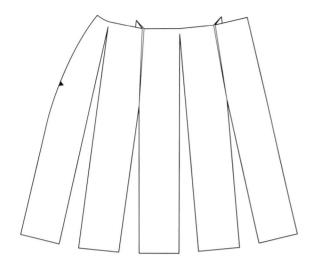

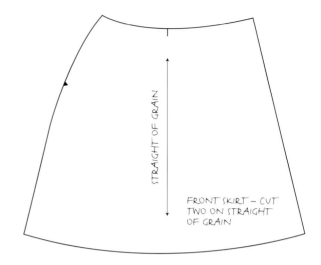

STRAIGHT OF GRAIN

FRONT SKIRT – CUT
TWO ON STRAIGHT
OF GRAIN

10 Cut up the two lines that go through the waist darts to the points of the dart and fold darts out. Cut up the other lines to within 2mm (⅛ in) of the waist and fan the sections out; in this sample the gaps are 4cm (1½ in).

11 Overlay the pattern with a new piece of drafting paper and trace it, drawing in a new hem line. Add 1.5cm (⅝ in) seam allowances, the same amount for the hem and relevant pattern markings.

12 To make the back skirt of the dress, overlay the basic skirt back block with drafting paper and trace it. Draw in a vertical line running through the waist dart and one through the middle of the pattern piece. Cut the lines and fold out the dart as for the front skirt.

13 Fan the lines out as for the front skirt to create the flare.

14 Add 1.5cm (⅝ in) seam allowances and the same amount for the hem. Add relevant pattern markings and label the section 'back skirt – cut one on the fold'.

shaped hem

You can give this dress a fresh twist by altering the hem shape on the wrap-over section of the skirt. Cut the pattern as for Steps 7–10. Trace it as in Step 11, but along the hem stop about 30cm (12 in) from the front edge. On the front edge, trace down to the same distance from the hem. Draw in a smooth curve to create the new shape.

Turn this summer day dress into a sophisticated outfit for a wedding by making it from mediumweight linen and adding elegant bell sleeves.

princess-line dress

This is a classic style that can be used to create anything from a little black party dress to a smart dress for the office.

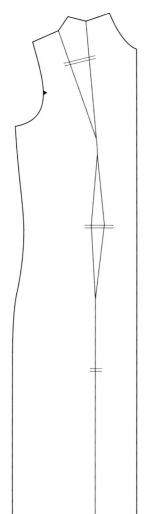

1 Overlay the basic dress front block (see page 58) with drafting paper and trace the centre front section, following the right-hand side of the shoulder-to-bust dart. Draw a line between the tip of this dart and the waistline dart, then trace down the right-hand side of the waistline dart. Draw a straight vertical line, running parallel to the centre front line, from the tip of this dart to the hem.

2 Trace the side section of the dress, following the left-hand side of the darts, then the line drawn Step 1.

3 Draw balance lines across the width of both darts; these will be helpful whem it comes to making up the dress.

added flare

Additional flare can be added to the skirt by simply adding extra width at the hem and re-drawing the seams from the waist to meet the new hem line. You may need to curve the hem slightly to make it hang well; turn to Flared Skirt (see page 92) to see how the hem on that pattern has been adjusted for the added flare.

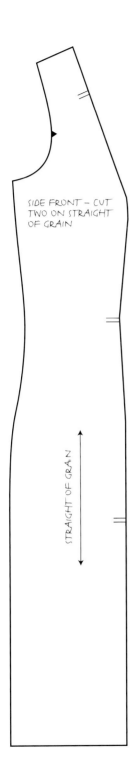

SIDE FRONT – CUT TWO ON STRAIGHT OF GRAIN

STRAIGHT OF GRAIN

4 Add 1.5cm (⅝ in) seam allowances, a 5cm (2 in) hem and relevant pattern markings to the side front piece of the pattern.

5 Add 1.5cm (⅝ in) seam allowances, a 5cm (2 in) hem and relevant pattern markings to the centre front piece of the pattern.

6 Repeat this process for the back of the dress. If you plan to fit a centre back zip, then the back centre section will have to be cut in two pieces. However, if you intend to fit a side underarm zip, then the back section can be cut on the fold.

7 If you are not adding sleeves to the dress, then create a neck and armhole facing in one section (see page 118-119).

CENTRE FRONT

CENTRE FRONT – CUT ONE ON THE FOLD

seaming

To sew the curved princess seams over the bust, first mark the balance marks you drew in Step 3 on the fabric with tailor's tacks (see page 20). Take the time to pin and tack the seam accurately, matching the tailor's tacks, or when you machine-sew the seam will not lie smooth.

Sundress with Straps

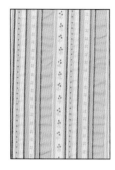

This is a perfect dress for summer days or evenings out, with a shawl draped over your shoulders just in case there is a chill in the air.

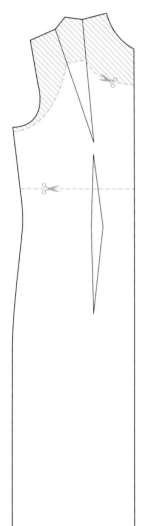

1 To make the dress front, overlay the basic dress front block (see page 58) with drafting paper and trace it. Work out how low you want the neckline to be and mark this on the centre front line.

2 Work out how high you want the strap to be placed on the dart line.

3 Drop the armhole slightly then draw in design line. Work out where the under bust line will be and draw that in. If you want the dress to be a little tighter across the bust, then alter the side seams as for the sun top with straps (see pages 76–79). Cut along the design lines.

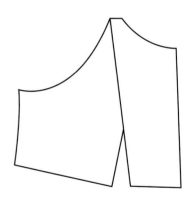

4 Cut up from the top of the lower bust dart (the top of the waist dart on the original dress pattern) to within 2mm (⅛ in) of the bottom of the shoulder-to-bust dart. Fold out the shoulder-to-bust dart. Re-draw the dart so that the point ends where the original lower-bust dart ended, otherwise the point of the dart will be too high.

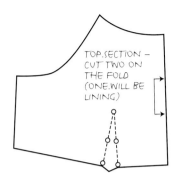

TOP.SECTION —
CUT TWO ON
THE FOLD
(ONE.WILL BE
LINING)

5 Overlay the pattern with a new piece of drafting paper and trace it. Add 1.5cm (⅝ in) seam allowances and relevant pattern markings.

lining the top

To self-line a section of a pattern, such as the front top in this instance, place the main piece and the lining piece right sides together. Taking a 1.5cm (⅝ in) seam allowance, machine-sew around the top edge. Clip the curves (see page 25), turn the piece right side out and press the sewn edge flat. Make up the pattern treating the lined section as one piece.

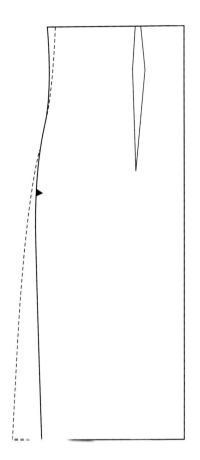

6 Add optional flare to the hem of the skirt section, as shown by the dotted line. Take an amount that is equal to the waist dart from the side seam, then just ignore the dart when making up the dress. However, if you prefer more shaping around the waist, leave the dart in place.

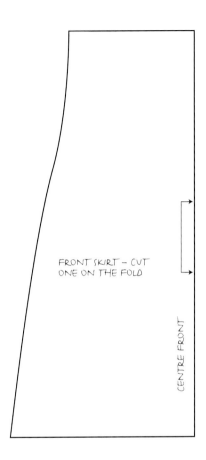

FRONT SKIRT — CUT ONE ON THE FOLD

CENTRE FRONT

7 Overlay the pattern with a new piece of drafting paper and trace it. Add 1.5cm (⅝ in) seam allowances, a 5cm (2 in) hem and relevant pattern markings.

continued next page ➤ ➤ ➤

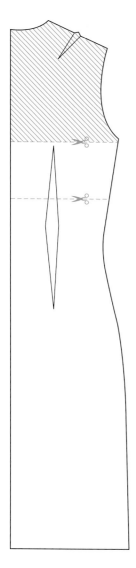

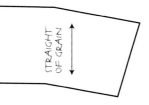

9 Cut along the design lines and fold out the dart on the back top section. Overlay the pattern with a new piece of drafting paper and trace it. Add 1.5cm (⅝ in) seam allowances and relevant pattern markings. Label the section 'back top – cut two on the fold (one will become lining)'.

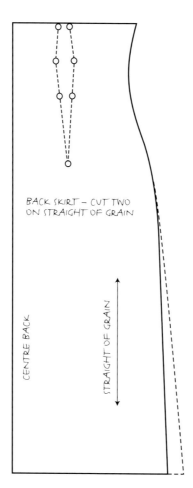

BACK SKIRT – CUT TWO
ON STRAIGHT OF GRAIN

CENTRE BACK

STRAIGHT OF GRAIN

10 Add optional flare to the hem of the skirt as for the front. Add 1.5cm (⅝ in) seam allowances, a 5cm (2 in) hem and relevant pattern markings.

11 If you want to insert the zip centre back, then the back top and skirt sections will both need to be cut in two pieces. If the zip is to be placed under the arm in the side seam, then cut both sections as one piece.

12 Measure how long you need the straps to be. Draw a rectangle that is the measured length and double the width you wish the finished strap to be.

13 Add 1.5cm (⅝ in) seam allowances and label the section 'straps – cut two on straight of grain'.

8 To make the dress back, overlay the basic dress back block with drafting paper and trace it. Drop the armhole by the same amount as for the front and draw a line straight across the back. Draw the under bust line in the same position as for the front.

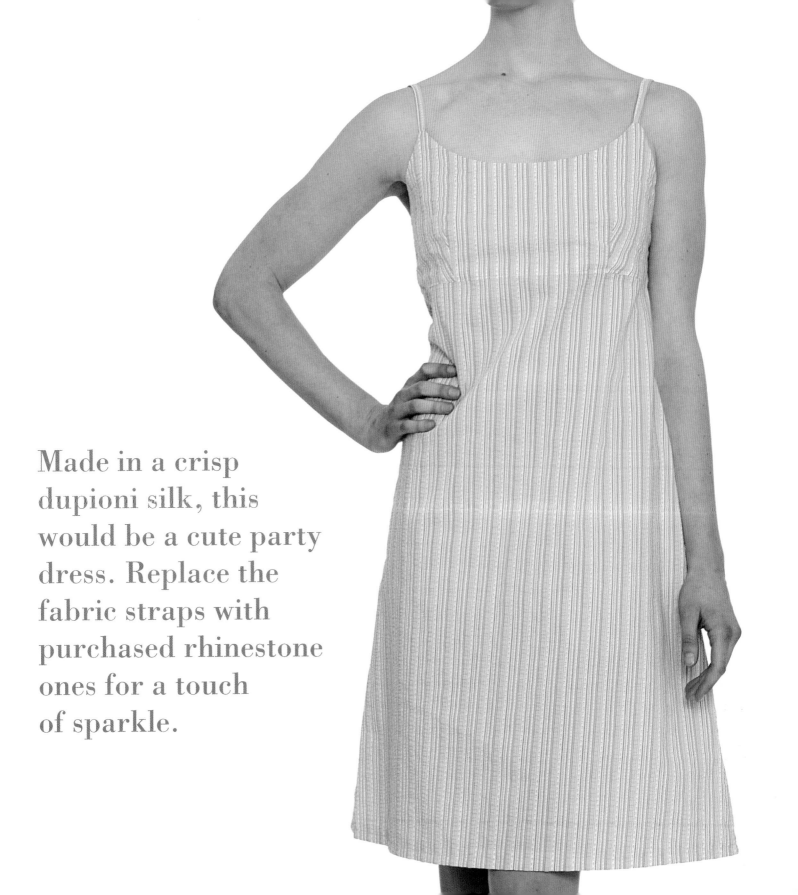

Made in a crisp dupioni silk, this would be a cute party dress. Replace the fabric straps with purchased rhinestone ones for a touch of sparkle.

flared dress

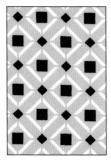

This flattering dress also looks great teamed with the Bell Sleeve or Flared Sleeve (see pages 84 and 89).

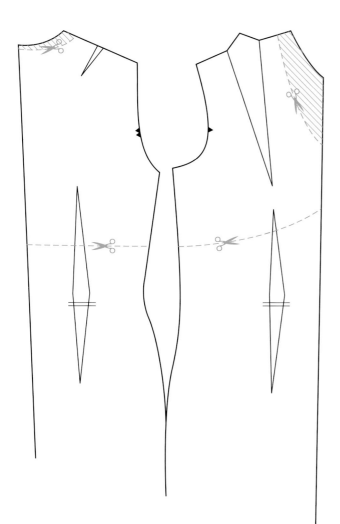

1 Overlay the basic dress front and back blocks (see page 58) with drafting paper and trace them. Work out where you want the under bust line to be on the front, mark it on the side seam and centre front line.

2 Draw in the under bust line, curving up from the side seam to the centre front line, as shown by the blue dotted line.

3 Mark the same point on the back side seam and draw a line straight across the back block.

4 Work out how low you wish the 'V' neckline to be. Starting a short way along the shoulder line, draw in the neck.

5 Redraw the back neck line, starting at the same position on the shoulder line as for front. Draw balance marks across the waist dart. Cut along the new design lines. The back bodice pattern does not need further alteration.

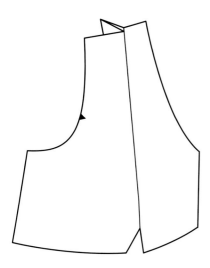

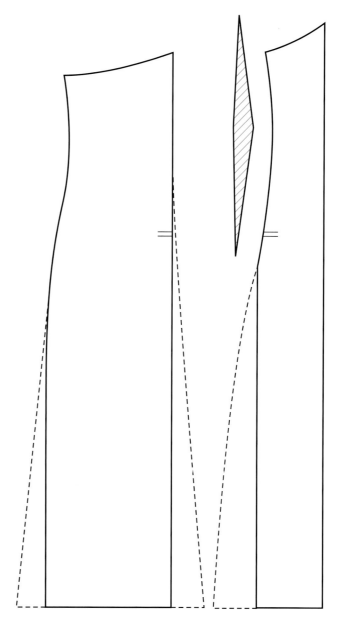

6 On the front bodice, cut up the centre of the lower bust dart (the waist dart on the original dress pattern) to the point of the shoulder-to-bust dart and fold out the shoulder-to-bust dart.

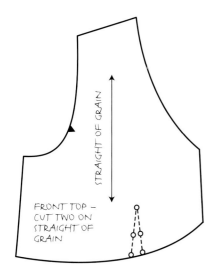

STRAIGHT OF GRAIN

FRONT TOP –
CUT TWO ON
STRAIGHT OF
GRAIN

7 Overlay the pattern with a new piece of drafting paper and trace it. Add 1.5cm (⅝ in) seam allowances and relevant pattern markings.

8 On the front skirt section of the dress, draw a line, parallel to the centre front line, running down the centre of the waistline dart to the hem. Cut up this line from the hem then cut either side of the dart, removing it from the pattern.

9 Add flare to the hem on both pattern pieces, as shown by the dotted line. The amount added is a personal choice.

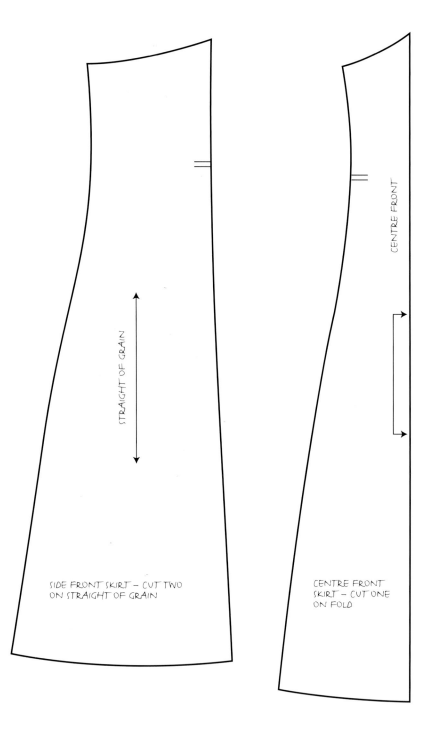

STRAIGHT OF GRAIN

SIDE FRONT SKIRT – CUT TWO
ON STRAIGHT OF GRAIN

CENTRE FRONT

CENTRE FRONT
SKIRT – CUT ONE
ON FOLD

10 Overlay the patterns with new pieces of drafting paper and trace them. Add 1.5cm (⅝ in) seam allowances, a 5cm (2 in) hem and relevant pattern markings.

11 Repeat Steps 8–10 with the back skirt section of the pattern.

12 If the dress is to be sleeveless, then cut duplicate bodice sections and use them as facings. If you are going to fit sleeves, then make neck and armhole facings (see pages 118-119) or neaten with bias binding (see pages 28-29).

facings

If you do not have enough fabric to cut facings from, choose a fabric in a similar colour or a shade lighter. Don't use a darker colour as it may affect the look of the main fabric.

The clean, simple lines of this dress make it a great candidate for further embellishment. Add a decorative braid around the hem or trim the neckline with sew-on motifs to add unique style.

extra elements

Some of your garments will need additional pieces, such as waistbands or facings. You may also want to add pockets or collars, or change the shape of a neckline. This chapter contains general instructions for these extra elements.

Pockets

Facings

Necklines

Waistbands

Cuffs

Collars

pockets

Three types of pocket are shown here: patch pockets, side-seam pockets and jeans-style front pockets.

Patch pocket

These versatile pockets can be made to any size and be put onto any garment. The measurements used here can be adjusted to suit design and taste.

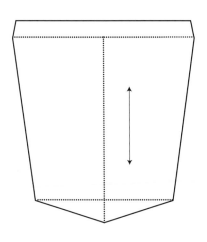

1 Draw a horizontal straight line 15cm (6 in) long.

2 At the centre point draw a vertical line running downwards for 15cm (6 in).

3 From the bottom of this vertical line, measure up 2.5cm (1 in) and draw a horizontal line 12.5cm (5 in) long, placing it centrally across the vertical line. These are the construction lines for a basic pocket.

4 Draw out the shape of the pocket, as shown.

5 Add 1cm (⅜ in) seam allowances to the side and bottom edges and 1.5cm (⅝ in) seam allowance along the top edge. This allows the top edge to be double turned to encase all raw edges and give a neater finish.

6 Add a straight of grain pattern marking and label the section 'pocket – cut two', assuming you require two matching pockets.

Side seam pocket

These are illustrated here on trousers, but the same principles apply for skirts and dresses. These pockets can be made in a lightweight fabric to reduce bulk in the side seams.

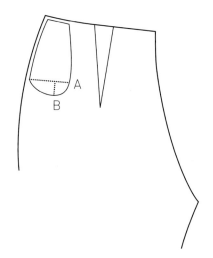

1 Overlay the basic trouser front block with a piece of drafting paper. Trace 10cm (4 in) along the waistline and 25cm (10 in) down the side seam.

2 From the bottom of the traced section of the side seam, draw a 15cm (6 in) horizontal line running towards the centre front line. Mark the end of this line point A.

3 From the side seam, measure 10cm (4 in) along this line. Draw a vertical line 5cm (2 in) long and mark the end point B.

4 Draw a curve from the end of the traced section of the side seam, down to point B then back up to point A.

5 Draw a gently curving line, as shown, up from point A to the end of the traced section of the waistline.

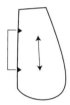

6 Add a straight of grain pattern marking and label the section 'pocket – cut two'. If you require a pocket in both side seams, then mark it 'cut four'.

7 The seam allowance on the pocket bag has been included in the drafting but a 1.5cm (⅝ in) seam allowance should be added along the side seam edge. On this edge, put a balance mark 7.5cm (3 in) from the top and 2.5cm (1 in) from the bottom to indicate the length of the opening.

Jeans-style front pocket
This pocket works on skirts and trousers, but not on dresses.

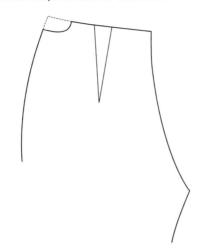

1 Overlay the basic trouser front block with a piece of drafting paper. Measure 10cm (4 in) along the waistline and 6cm (2⅜ in) down the side seam.

2 Draw a curved line, as shown, for the pocket opening. Then trace the rest of the trouser block.

jeans pockets

These are the most difficult style of pocket to make, but they are useful. If you find it tricky to understand them, a close look at the front pockets on your jeans will help you understand how they go together

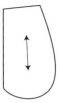

3 To create the first section of the pocket bag, draft the pocket as described for Side Seam Pocket, but measure 12.5cm (5 in) along the waistline rather than 10cm (4 in). Remember that this section will show on the completed garment, so you might want to make it in the same fabric as the main pieces.

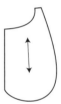

4 To create the second section of the pocket bag, place the first section in place on the trouser block. Lay a new piece of drafting paper over these two pattern blocks and carefully trace around the first pocket bag section and the curved pocket opening.

5 Add a straight of grain pattern marking and label the section 'pocket – cut two', assuming you require two matching pockets.

6 Included in the drafted pattern are seam allowances of 1cm (⅜ in) on the curve of the pocket opening and 1.5cm (⅝ in) on the rest of the pocket

facings

For a more professional finish to your garments use neck and armhole facings rather than hemming or binding. Facings are quick and simple to draft and are made from the same fabric as the rest of the garment.

Neckline facings are best created using a pattern without a dart along the shoulder line. If your pattern has the dart in this position then you will need to throw the dart to the side seam (see page 55).

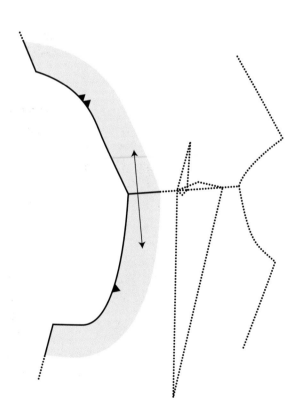

Armhole facing

Use this facing for a neat finish to the armholes on any style of sleeveless top.

1 Lay out the front bodice and back bodice patterns, matching the shoulder lines. If there are seam allowances on the pieces, fold them in so that they are not included in the facing pattern. Lay a new piece of drafting paper over the patterns. Trace around the armhole curves and 7.5cm (3 in) down the side seams.

2 Measure in 7.5cm (3 in) from the armhole curve at various points, then join the measured points to establish the outer curve, as shown by the tinted section on this pattern.

3 Add a 1cm (³⁄₈ in) seam allowance to the outer curve and a 1.5cm (⁵⁄₈ in) seam allowance to the side seam and armhole edges. Add a straight of grain pattern marking and label the section 'armhole facing – cut two'.

Standard neckline facing

This is the facing for the round neckline made when draping your basic bodice block (see pages 34–41).

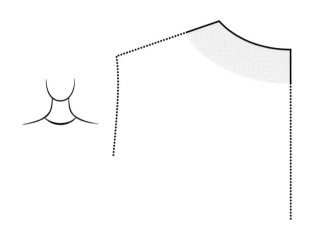

One-piece armhole and neckline facing

This is a neat solution for a sleeveless, collarless bodice and the neckline shape can be varied.

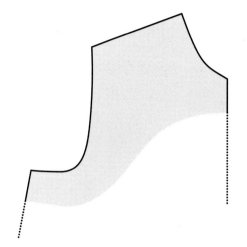

1 Lay a new piece of drafting paper over the front bodice block. Trace around the neck curve, 7.5cm (3 in) along the shoulder line and 7.5cm (3 in) down the centre front line.

2 Measure in 7.5cm (3 in) from the armhole curve at various points, then join the measured points to establish the outer curve, as shown by the tinted section on this pattern.

3 Add a 1cm (⅜ in) seam allowance to the outer curve and a 1.5cm (⅝ in) seam allowance to the side seam and neck edges. If the bodice has no front opening, then mark a 'place to fold line' along the centre front line and label the section 'neck facing – cut one to fold'. If there is a front opening, then add a 1.5cm (⅝ in) seam allowance to the centre front line.

4 Repeat the process for the back bodice neckline.

1 Lay a new piece of drafting paper over the front bodice block. Trace around the armhole curve, shoulder line and neck curve.

2 Trace 7.5cm (3 in) down the centre front line and the same measurement down the side seam. Measure in 7.5cm (3 in) from the bottom of the armhole curve and begin to draw around the lower edge of the armhole curve.

3 Curve the line around to the neck to meet the line coming down from the centre front, as shown by the tinted section on this pattern.

4 Add a 1cm (⅜ in) seam allowance to the lower curve and a 1.5cm (⅝ in) seam allowance to the side seam, neck, armhole and shoulder line edges. If the bodice has no front opening, then mark a 'place to fold line' along the centre front line and label the section 'front facing – cut one to fold'. If there is a front opening, then add a 1.5cm (⅝ in) seam allowance to the centre front line.

5 Repeat the process for the back bodice neckline.

necklines

The basic bodice neckline can be altered to suit both taste and current trends by simply changing the shape. Here are facings for three popular neckline shapes without a front opening.

Square neckline

A classic neckline shape that looks good on both daytime and evening wear.

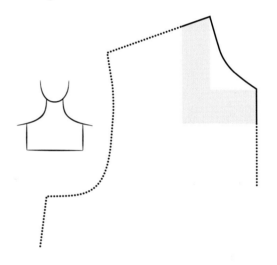

1 Lay a new piece of drafting paper over the front bodice block. Draw a vertical line running down from the shoulder point. Draw a line across at right angles to meet the centre front line, just below the original neck line.

2 Trace the complete bodice block. This is the new front block with a square neckline.

3 To draft a facing, place a new piece of paper over the pattern and trace the new neckline. Measure 7.5cm (3 in) along the shoulder line and the same amount down the centre front line. Draw in the outer edge of the facing, as shown by the tinted section on this pattern.

4 Add a 1cm (⅜ in) seam allowance to the outer edge and a 1.5cm (⅝ in) seam allowance to the shoulder line and neck edge. Mark a 'place to fold line' along the centre front line and label the section 'neck facing – cut one to fold'.

back neck facings

When creating a front neck facing you will almost always have to create a back neck facing. This will usually keep to the original curve of the back neck, though the shoulder line will need to be shortened to match the front.

'V' neckline

A timeless neckline shape that flatters most figures. The 'V' can be cut as low or as high as desired.

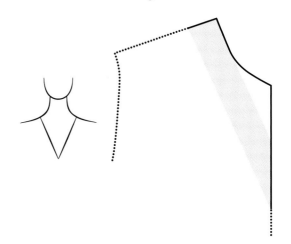

1   Lay a new piece of drafting paper over the front bodice block. Mark on the centre front line the point where the 'V' neckline is to finish. Place the rule on this point and draw a straight line to the shoulder point.

2   Trace the complete bodice block. This is the new front pattern with a deep 'V' neckline.

3   To draft a facing, place a new piece of paper over the pattern and trace the new neckline. Measure 7.5cm (3 in) along the shoulder line and the same measurement down the centre front line. Measure in 7.5cm (3 in) from the straight line forming the edge of the 'V' and join these three points to establish the outer edge, as shown by the tinted section on this pattern.

4   Add a 1cm (³/₈ in) seam allowance to the outer edge and a 1.5cm (⁵/₈ in) seam allowance to the shoulder line and neck edge. Mark a 'place to fold line' along the centre front line and label the section 'neck facing – cut one to fold'.

Deeply curved neckline

This neckline can be cut as low as you wish, or dare!

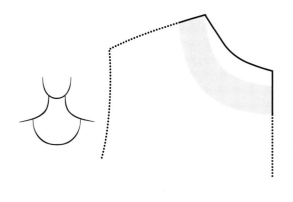

1   Lay a new piece of drafting paper over the front bodice block. Curve the neckline as desired, working to the measurement taken from the base of the neck to the desired neckline depth.

2   Trace the complete bodice block. This is the new front block with a deeply curved neckline.

3   To draft a facing, place a new piece of paper over the pattern and trace the new neckline. Measure 7.5cm (3 in) along the shoulder line and the same measurement down the centre front line.

4   Measure in 7.5cm (3 in) from the neckline at various points, then join the measured points to establish the outer curve, as shown by the tinted section on this pattern.

5   Add a 1cm (³/₈ in) seam allowance to the outer edge and a 1.5cm (⁵/₈ in) seam allowance to the shoulder line and neck edge. Mark a 'place to fold line' along the centre front line and label the section 'neck facing – cut one to fold'.

Waistbands

Skirts and trousers will need a waistband to finish them off. You can use either a straight, visible band or a self-faced one that lies inside the garment and does not show.

Straight waistband

This is the basic and simplest type of waistband. The width can be adjusted to suit taste and fashion.

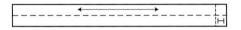

1 Draw a rectangle measuring 10cm (4 in) wide and the same length as the waist measurement, plus 2.5cm (1 in). The additional 2.5cm (1 in) is to accommodate the buttonhole and can be adjusted in length to suit.

2 Draw a line along the middle of this rectangle; this will be the centre fold line.

3 Mark the position of the buttonhole within the 2.5cm (1 in) that was added to the waist measurement.

4 Along all four edges add 1.5cm (⅝ in) seam allowances and add a straight of grain line. Label the section 'waistband – cut one on straight of grain in fabric and one in interfacing'.

Self-faced waistband

This style of waistband works well with garments that have a lot of waist shaping.

1 Lay a new piece of drafting paper over the skirt/trouser front block. Carefully trace the waistline, the front dart and a short distance along the side seam and the centre front seam.

2 Every 2.5cm (1 in), measure down 5cm (2 in) from the waistline and make a mark. Join these marks to create a band across the top of the skirt/trousers.

3 Cut out this band then fold out the dart.

4 Lay a new piece of drafting paper over the pattern and trace the facing. Add 1.5cm (⅝ in) seam allowances to both long edges and the side seam edge. Mark a 'place to fold line' along the centre front line and label the section 'waistband – cut one to fold in fabric and one in interfacing'. If the skirt or trousers you have designed have a front zip fastening rather than a side opening, then the front facing is marked with a straight of grain line and labeled 'cut two'.

5 Repeat the process for the back of the skirt/trousers.

Cuffs

Some sleeve styles require a cuff, and there are two basic types to choose from; a button-fastening cuff and a band cuff. The widths of both can be adjusted to suit. Turn to page 26 for instructions for sewing a cuff.

Band cuff

This style of cuff has to be slipped over the hand to get the garment on.

1 Measure around the widest part of the hand. Draw a rectangle that is this length and 10cm (4 in) wide.

2 Draw a line along the middle of this rectangle, this will be the centre fold line.

3 Along all four edges add 1.5cm (⅝ in) seam allowances then label the section 'cuff – cut two on straight of grain in fabric and two in interfacing'.

Cuff with buttonhole

This cuff can be opened to let the hand pass through and so can be fitted tightly around the wrist.

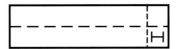

1 Draw a rectangle measuring 10cm (4 in) wide and the same length as the wrist measurement, plus 2.5cm (1 in). The additional 2.5cm (1 in) is to accommodate the buttonhole and can be adjusted in length to suit.

2 Draw a line along the middle of this rectangle, this will be the centre fold line.

3 Mark the position of the buttonhole within the 2.5cm (1 in) that was added to the wrist measurement.

4 Along all four edges add 1.5cm (⅝ in) seam allowances then label the section 'cuff – cut two on straight of grain in fabric and two in interfacing'.

cuff style

You can be creative with cuffs and make them in a toning, or even contrasting, colour fabric to the main garment. Or use a commercial covered button kit and cover it with the garment fabric to add a designerly finishing touch to your outfit.

Collars

Sometimes a garment needs finishing with something other than a plain neckline. What better way than adding an interesting collar? Turn to page 27 for instructions for sewing a collar. The following directions and diagrams show bodices without button fronts or openings. If the neck opening is not large enough to go over the head, then an opening must be introduced or the neckline must be enlarged.

Band collar
A very simple collar that is easy to draft and sew.

1 To ensure that this collar is comfortable to wear, drop the bodice centre back line by 1cm (³⁄₈ in) and the centre front line by 2.5cm (1 in), then redraw the neckline on the bodice. Once this has been done, measure the new neckline.

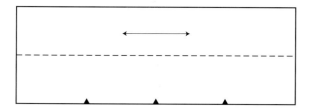

▲ 2 Draw a rectangle the same length as the neckline measurement and twice as deep as the required finished height of the collar. Draw a line along the middle of this rectangle, this will be the centre fold line.

3 On the bodice patterns, measure the distance from the shoulder line to the centre front, the centre front line to the opposite shoulder line and the shoulder line to the centre back. Mark these measurements on the collar as they will make fitting it easier.

4 Along all four edges add 1.5cm (⁵⁄₈ in) seam allowances and add a straight of grain line. Label the section 'collar – cut one on straight of grain in fabric and one in interfacing'.

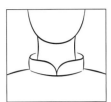

Mandarin collar
A classic style of collar that never seems to go out of fashion.

1 To ensure that this collar is comfortable to wear, drop the bodice centre front line by 1.5cm (⅝ in) then redraw the neckline on the bodice. Once this has been done, measure the new neckline.

2 Draw a rectangle the same length as the neckline measurement and as deep as the required finished height of the collar. Curve ends for shaping (if desired), ensuring both ends are the same.

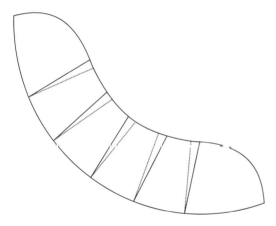

▲3 For the collar to sit close to the neck it must be curved slightly. To do this, make five equally spaced cuts along the top edge, cutting down to within 2mm (⅛ in) of the bottom edge. Overlap the edges of each cut by 5mm (¼ in) and pin in place.

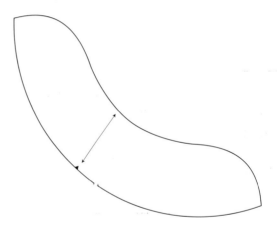

▲4 Lay a new piece of drafting paper over the pattern and trace it. If you wish, curve the top edges of the centre fronts, as shown.

5 Add 1.5cm (⅝ in) seam allowances all around and a straight of grain line. Label the section 'collar – cut two on straight of grain in fabric and one in interfacing'. One of the fabric pieces will be the under collar.

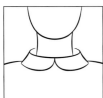

Peter Pan collar
This collar style looks great on adults and children.

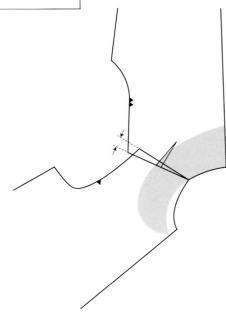

1 Lay out the front and back bodice with the shoulder lines meeting at the neck and overlapping 1.5cm (⅝ in) at the shoulders. (If your pattern includes seam allowances, fold them under so that they are not included in the drafting.)

2 Lay a new piece of drafting paper over the patterns. To ensure that this collar is comfortable to wear, the bodice neckline has to be redrawn. To do this, work around the neck line starting at the centre back line dropping down 3mm (⅛ in) then at the centre front dropping down 1.5cm (⅝ in).

3 Begin to draw in the new neckline starting at the centre back line. Once the midway point along the front neck line is reached, begin to draw down to the point marked on the centre front line. Redraw the bodice.

4 Lay a new piece of drafting paper over the pattern. Decide how wide you want the collar to be and measure and mark this width every 2.5cm (1 in) around the neckline.

5 Following the marks, draw a smooth line for the edge of the collar.

6 Just before the centre front line, begin to curve the collar line up towards the neck point.

7 Remove 5mm (¼ in) from the centre back line; this is to adjust for the increase in neck size when you dropped 1.5cm (⅝ in) at the centre front line.

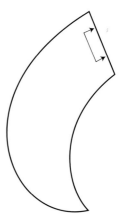

8 Add 1.5cm (⅝ in) seam allowances all around and a fold mark on the centre back line. Label the section 'collar – cut two on fold in fabric and one in interfacing'. One of the fabric pieces will be the under collar.

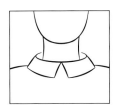

Eton collar

This is a great alternative to a Peter Pan collar and works very well on more formal tops.

1 Lay out the front and back bodice with the shoulder lines meeting at the neck and overlapping 1.5cm (⅝ in) at the shoulders. (If your pattern includes seam allowances, fold them under so that they are not included in the drafting.)

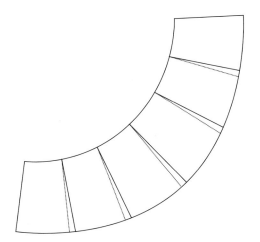

2 Lay a new piece of drafting paper over the patterns. To ensure that this collar is comfortable to wear, drop the centre back neck 3mm (⅛ in) and the centre front 1.5cm (⅝ in).

3 Draw in the new neckline starting at the centre back line. Once the midway point along the front neck line has been reached, begin to draw down to the new position. Trace the rest of the bodice.

4 Lay a new piece of drafting paper over the pattern. Decide how wide you want the collar to be and measure and mark this width every 2.5cm (1 in) around the neckline.

5 Following the marks, draw a smooth line for the edge of the collar.

6 Remove 5mm (¼ in) from the centre back line; this is to adjust for the increase in neck size when you dropped 1.5cm (⅝ in) at the centre front line.

7 Divide the pattern into six equal parts and cut from the outer line to within 2mm (⅛ in) of the inner line.

8 Overlap the edges of each cut by 5mm (¼ in) and pin in place. Lay a new piece of drafting paper over the pattern and trace it.

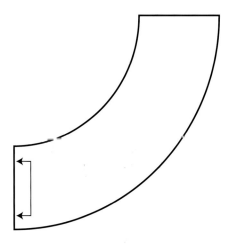

9 Add 1.5cm (⅝ in) seam allowances all around and a fold mark on the centre back line. Label the section 'collar – cut two on fold in fabric and one in interfacing'. One of the fabric pieces will be the under collar.

index

acknowledgements

I would like to thank the following for their invaluable help in making the garments in this book: Jackie Cilia, a good friend, whose pinning, tacking, pressing and attaching of interfacing skills are second to none, and Barbara Mascetti for her sewing skills. Thanks to Paula Breslich for commissioning the book, Kate Haxell for being a BF editor, Louise Leffler for great design, Dominic Harris for lovely photos and Stephen Dew for clear illustrations.